]

The hard
it appear
with *Pocket Guide to your He♥rt*. There are such important messages held within the simplicity of the words and exercises. Many people will be dismissive of its simplicity, yet sadly, it is just those people (like me) who need to read it and practice it.

Life is a constant reminder of how little one knows just when you start to believe you know more. I thought after writing my first book that I had found the answers, it was only as life took me down new roads did I realize I had only understood the past, and not the present or the future me. In some ways it is easier to write a book than practice its message, just like it is often easier to help other people than yourself. The beauty of this book is empowerment of the reader to be able to take control of their own pain and damage in a relatively easy way.

*Patrick Ellis, Author—*Breakthrough *and* Dying In Love

A woman with cancer said to me, "There's no testimony without the test." Having known Colleen for more than two decades, I have witnessed her 'tests' and search for a method that healed a weary and (seemingly) broken heart. She found it! ... so simple you can do it anywhere, anytime.. and no one will know you're doing it ... but they'll witness the shift from the unbearable burden of anger, fear and resentment to the bearable lightness of a heart filled with love, forgiveness and hope. Are you ready for all the love and peace you can stand?

Joey Schooley, Actor, Spokesperson

I have found *Pocket Guide to your He♥rt* practice changed how I look at life. I came to realize that in order to go forward in life you sometimes have to go backwards. It has shown me how to accept not being the perfect little girl and to learn to like me for me. Using these formulas I am putting my life back together again one step at a time.

Mary-Lee Barker, Executive Legal Assistant

The inner workout is a real confidence-booster! Knowing that I can deal with emotional issues simply by spending time understanding the origins of my feelings, and then being able to change my response accordingly, has made a big difference in my life. Now I feel more in control, and at the same time, more open to change.

Helen Smith, Communications Director,
Manulife Reinsurance

Colleen thank you for teaching me the meaning of true love, and just how I can light the way on our journey of healing, if we are prepared to let the light in.

The work Colleen has done with me has been invaluable in embracing my inner child—she has made me a much more authentic friend, parent and leader, to inspire others to find their voice in the work place to become all that they are. Everyday I am becoming more and more all that I am.

Her care and attention with my daughters has helped their passage from adolescence into womanhood immensely. They, too, are becoming more and more who they are, with balance and harmony.

Carolyn Roberts. President Local 2137,
Canadian Union of Public Employees

Just meeting Colleen has changed my life in so many ways. Her peaceful, open hearted nature made me feel safe enough to start my own journey to peace.

My journey led me to accepting the person I am and to taking responsibility for my misbehaviors and anger—it has made me a more patient and loving wife, mother, sister, friend and daughter. Without *Pocket Guide to your He♥rt* formulas I have no doubt that my marriage would be in serious trouble eventually. My anger and resentment would have led me to being a victim for the rest of my life and I would have damaged all the relationships I so deeply care about.

Patricia Suffield, Dental Sales Representative,
Wife, Mother

Pocket Guide to your He♥rt

Pocket Guide to your He♥rt

Colleen Hoffman Smith

Heart Bridge Publishing

2003 • Toronto, Canada

Published in 2003 by Heart Bridge Publishing
P.O. Box 67063, South Common PO,
Mississauga, Ontario, Canada L5L 5V4

www.pocketguidetoyourheart.com

National Library of Canada Cataloguing in Publication

Smith, Colleen Hoffman, 1953-
Pocket guide to your heart : three formulas to keep you
authentic & attractive / Colleen Hoffman Smith, author ;
Nancy Newman, illustrator.

ISBN 0-9734020-0-8

1. Self-help techniques. I. Title.

BF632.S55 2003   158.1   C2003-905611-2

Cover and illustrations: Nancy Newman
Cover photo: Yanka and Henk Van der Kolk
Imaging and Photography
Print and production management: Karen Petherick,
Intuitive Design International Ltd.

Printed and Bound in Canada

… My mother and father, Susan and Phillip Hoffman. Thank you for teaching me unconditional love. I am who I am because of your love. You created a safe family foundation to grow from within. I love you from my soul.

… Lindsay and Lauren, my amazing daughters, you are the reflection of the light in my life and remind me each day of love. I am always proud of who you are. Thank you for choosing me to be your mom, it has been my greatest joy. You are the wind beneath my wings.

… Jessica, my precious stepdaughter, we fell in love the moment we met. You remind me each day how magical life is. You are an angel.

… Bruce, my beloved husband and soulmate. You inspire me to be all that I am each moment. Thank you for creating a safe place for me to heal and expand my love more. You are the perfect partner for me. You are enchanted love.

… My triplet sisters Frannie and Philomene, thank you for reminding me to breathe since birth. I see all the parts of me in you. Philomene, your wisdom keeps me grounded and Frannie, your insights and truth inspire me to fly. Steve, Luke and Lane, how blessed I am to have you in my life.

… Philip, my brother, you speak to my soul without words. You have inspired my search for peace. Janine and Jessie, you have sparked our family with your presence.

… To my extended family, Bob and Joan Smith, you are my second parents. Your loving hearts encourage me with care and understanding. Dave and Noelle, Meaghan Bronwyn and Sarah Smith, Stu and Helen, Michelle and Kevin Smith, you have all brought family joy to my life.

To my entire family
And beloved relatives.
I am in Love
With you in my life
Forever

CONTENTS

ACKNOWLEDGEMENTS

I have so many friends in my life who support me unconditionally and inspire me endlessly. My life journey continues to open many doors attracting incredible relationships that contribute to my own personal and professional evolution and with the success of *Pocket Guide to your He♥rt*.

My appreciation to Karen Petherick for your talent and creative process that guided *Pocket Guide to your He♥rt* to fruition. You made the editing and publishing process painless. You are an enlightened professional and forever friend. I am so blessed to have Nancy Newman illustrate *Pocket Guide to your He♥rt*. Nancy your magnificent artistry together with your wisdom danced on the pages of my book. Thank you for helping me share this message with the world.

I am grateful for Jo-Anne Cutler, my business manager and friend, your commitment and unfailing belief in my message has connected our purpose. I acknowledge Harvey Diamond for your constant inspiration and valuable message for all humanity.

I am deeply grateful for my Goddess friends who dance with me through the fires, never doubting our soul connection. Linda Ginou your friendship and love has been woven in my heart forever. Thank you for your unconditional love and support with everything that I do. Carolyn Roberts, our daughters connected our hearts and our friendship grows with the gardens of our life. You have helped me embrace many parts of myself, I am deeply grateful. To Mary-Lee Barker, your friendship and encouragement has been so important to me. Donna Hamelin, your soft spirit stands on the sidelines quietly cheering me on, thank you. I express my gratitude to Karen King who believed in me and supported me in so many ways. You are a remarkable woman and friend who opened the door to my coaching career.

Judy McDowell, Haike Vaudry, Joey Schooley, Lily Colasanti and Lanee, our beautiful connections gently move me into the space of love, laughter and playfulness. Francesca Milano your heart always reminds me of the love, thank you for inspiring the title *Pocket Guide to your He♥rt*. Debra Taylor, it is so beautiful to see the love of your open heart sparkle through your eyes. Fabulous Yanka Van der Kolk your photography and imaging expertise has always astounded me, thank you for capturing my spirit with the camera, I love your friendship. I am forever grateful to Brenda Atkinson, Jo-Anne Cutler and Nancy Newman for your commitment to coaching with *Pocket Guide to your He♥rt* formulas. Thank you for our heart connection and for seeing the vision with me to inspire the world.

I have deep appreciation and love for Dave Benn, my children's beloved father. Thank you for always being there for us. To Dave's wife Liz, you are a wonderful step-mother. Thank you for loving and caring for our daughters like they are your own.

Goldlinx International was one of my greatest experiences because of these exceptional people. Charlotte Whaley you traveled with me across North America as we laughed and cried, expanding our dream. The foundation of our partnership was love and respect and our friendship never died. In memory of my beloved friend and mentor the late Forest Shaklee. I carry his wise words of inspiration in my heart. "If you are not in fear within, you will not feel fear in others. See each person as your friend not your enemy and inspire them to be the best they can be." Diana McLeod, Jennifer Childs, Rose Kynock and Ann Lee, your talent and loyalty will always be appreciated and I forever hold you in my heart. Thank you Thino Cacciolo, your respect, friendship and support will always be invaluable to me. Tricia Ryan, you are the best networker I know, I love our heart connection.

Gayle Gaynon, Richard Michna, Gord McMehen, Stephen Locke, Chuck Fry, Denny Mee, Ron Perera, Pam Pleger, Richard Perry, your wisdom and friendship always looked out for me. Your talents guided the ship in the sunshine and the storms, I am grateful.

With gratitude to the Goldlinx Leaders who touched the world with their hearts. I will never forget you.

To all of my clients who find the courage to go within, surrendering to the past, letting go, to heal their present. Your commitment to yourself and *Pocket Guide to your He♥rt* formulas, inspire me each day. I celebrate with you the dance of freedom.

FOREWORD

by Harvey Diamond (author of *Fit for Life*)

I have devoted my career to preventative health care with inner cleansing. The focus of my FIT FOR LIFE program has been on physical health and wellness through natural nutrition and care for the body.

There is emerging evidence that emotional cleansing is equally important for a comprehensive program to avoid illness that suppressed emotions can cause. Most of us have experienced the onset of physical illness at a time of vulnerability caused by emotional stress.

Colleen's book *Pocket Guide to your He♥rt* is an important tool that each of us can use to cleanse ourselves emotionally. I believe, to achieve a happier and fuller life, we need to find the inner peace that is an important part of our personal preventative health care.

Colleen's three simple formulas provide a method for anyone to connect with their self-worth and inner strength and to find the inner peace and joy we all long for in our lives. Her approach focuses on our ability to heal ourselves by taking responsibility for our own happiness. The key to her technique lies in the fundamental truth that the spirit we were each born with is pure light. Each of us can at anytime reveal that light by using her formula to remove the density and heaviness of past wounds, unfelt emotions and daily challenges.

From that wonderful self-connected place, you can **look** within to find your answers; you can then **live** in peace and fulfillment, instead of fear and negativity.

The result of this process of clearing the past resentments, suppressed hurts and uncomfortable emotions, is that everything can flow freely and easily with radiant attractive energy of peace and confidence.

Pocket Guide to your He♥rt program creates a support system for people to healthily take care of fears, angers, and disappointments. Once you release your uncomfortable feelings and let go, you will find that there is more space inside you that is lighter and healthier. This wonderful place of self-worth, love and peace will naturally **lead** and inspire others.

Pocket Guide to your He♥rt formulas provide three simple tools that anyone can use to bridge the inner connection to well-being and self-worth and a healthy relationship with yourself and your life. Emotional health is also **Fit for Life.**

Take care of your emotional body without MEDICATION.

All God's Blessings
Harvey Diamond

HARVEY DIAMOND is the co-author of the # 1 New York Times bestseller, FIT FOR LIFE, which has sold over 11 million copies worldwide and has been translated into 32 languages. Internationally known as an author, teacher, and health consultant, he has appeared on hundreds of radio and TV programs including Larry King Live, Oprah!, Nightline, *and* Good Morning America. *He lives in Sarasota, Florida. Harvey's recent book is called FIT FOR LIFE NOT FAT FOR LIFE.*

To find out more about Fit for Life or Harvey Diamond www.fitforlifetime.com.

As I went through my medical training, I came to realize that medicine is very good at diagnosing disease and providing treatment, however, what medicine seemed to lack was the capacity to actually heal, especially the emotional wounds that disease and illness can bring.

When I became critically ill myself, and my first child was stillborn, it became more painfully evident to me than ever that medicine was lacking in the capacity to heal the anger, resentment, and fear that I was left with as a result of my own illness.

There were days when I was paralyzed by the intense grief and anger over what I experienced. I didn't seem to be able to even access these feelings to deal with them with my therapist. When Colleen started working with me, I began to be able to feel and examine the emotional pain that was deep within my body. I began to release the feelings, and I started to feel peaceful again for the first time in months, maybe years. I found that I was able to more accurately express my feelings with my own therapist, and she provided me the bridge that was necessary to move forward with my medical treatment. After months of practice with Colleen's technique, along with receiving regular medical care from a psychiatrist, I finally reached a place of peace and forgiveness, and within days I became pregnant with my second child. I will continue to use these techniques to maintain emotional well being and balance. Pocket Guide to your He♥rt *has been an excellent complimentary practice to the medical care I receive, and has effectively bridged the gap between medical treatment and spiritual and emotional healing.*

Dr. Sarah Doig Pendergrast, MD

When you take dance lessons you may discover another way to do the tango that feels much more comfortable for you. In the beginning, your instructor teaches you different steps. It's awkward at first, but once you have practiced, the wonderful music moves you and your body feels good. When your dance partner is also comfortable and confident in the steps, you move together with strength—the passion is felt independently yet, together, it's beautiful to watch.

— ❤ —

When you start a new exercise program, your body is stretched in different ways and you release stress from many places. You work your muscles, build your heart rate and in time, the workout is an important part of your life. Your body starts to feel and look more attractive.

— ❤ —

When you find a healthy and compatible way of eating, it not only makes you feel satisfied but the joy you take in your meals makes you feel good. Your health is cared for on many levels when you eat well; looking great is a bonus. Your clothes fit better and your skin and hair are healthy.

The emotional body, your spirit, needs attention, too. My formulas, that consist of a daily practice, can help you connect to this important relationship with yourself and commit to a healthy body and spirit. They will also help you become more authentic and attractive.

My clients are put on a four-week program. They commit to four sessions, one week apart, and I am on call for them during this time—guiding them when their changed perception and new way of being feels uncomfortable and they need to be inspired to remember how to feel good again. The formulas and the practice I teach help my clients to reprogram themselves. It's no different than changing your eating habits, your exercise program, or committing to any course in life. The partnership is between you and the concept. The miracle lies in the change of perception or in the confirmation that the new technique or knowledge we have acquired feels right or comfortable. There are times when an instructor, a mentor or a guide can make any change easier.

My one-on-one sessions are very personal and individual, yet I have found that everyone's needs are similar. What makes us different is our behavior and misbehavior, our conscious and unconscious way of living.

We have been conditioned to behave a certain way when we feel uncomfortable. We respond and react without even thinking about it. If you find that you are tired of "wearing" yourself because the life you have attracted is not comfortable, it's because your soul, your emotional body is saying, **"I want to do it differently."** It's telling you to go "inside."

We can always exercise our free will to make choices; we can change our mind and do something different from the way we were conditioned. The world around us may behave a certain way … it doesn't mean we have to, especially when we realize we no longer feel comfortable.

So when you decide to change your mind, change your behavior, learn a new program and find your way to a better life, it's great to have a guide. I have never wanted anyone to become dependent on me to make them feel good. My desire is to teach people to have their own formulas and tools to find their own peace. These formulas have worked for me. The amazing friends who are my clients have been saying to me for years, "Colleen, I wish you were in my back pocket." That's why I decided to write *Pocket Guide to your He♥rt*.

You can read *Pocket Guide to your He♥rt* over a weekend and start practicing it immediately. You can carry it with you for a quick reference anytime you need to remind yourself. **We only forget long enough to remember**. Once you realize that it is entirely up to you to find your way back to peace, take responsibility and find that place each moment. Each day you can inspire others and teach the children that it is all inside us. And, if you forget, you can always open up *Pocket Guide to your He♥rt* to remind yourself again … and again … and again …

To be authentic and attractive.

Let's Connect

I started my personal journey of learning about who I was, who I am, and what I was becoming with the outer body "package." One of my many gifts from God was a good outer package to live with: great skin, healthy metabolism, beautiful hair and body complemented by a vibrant smile. With this package of mine I went into the modeling business. It's amazing to look back and see the doors we go through to gather experience and information for our future. The modeling business seemed to feed my confidence, but it left me with a false sense of security. My outer package and personality opened doors for me, but when it came to feeling good about myself, being confident in my ability to make decisions, I could easily be manipulated and controlled. So my journey to strengthen my self-worth was born from the many experiences that made me feel my lack of self-love. I only began to realize my talents and to appreciate my integrity as time went on.

In my younger days I realized I had another talent. That was my ease for being with people and for mirroring and inspiring their own self-love, their self-worth, and in holding onto the space for them so they could be all that they were. People thought that the goodness was only in me, but I knew anything they saw or felt when they were with me was also inside of them. It was easy for me to allow people to shine, to feel good about themselves, and this experience created a comfortable and inspiring moment for them, whether they were alone or in a group. This talent came naturally to me. In my younger days it wasn't clear to me how I could use this talent to know others and myself, and to create a safe place to experience what was going on inside us. As time went on I realized the importance of meeting each person or experience in my life without judgment or expectation.

I used my expertise and my talents to open a modeling school. For fourteen years I built a wonderful business, creating courses and teaching people of all ages how to look good and feel more confident. "*Sante bien dans ta peau*" is a phrase passed on to me by my mother, and means "To feel good in your skin." I've used this expression throughout my career when talking about feeling good about yourself and feeling good in your body. How you feel inside affects how you appear to others. "To feel good in your skin" refers to how your whole self feels.

I created courses that taught people how to get in

touch with their outer beauty, their fashionable, healthy image, and from this place they felt more comfortable about opening their hearts to their uniqueness. **The discovery of one's self.**

While I was teaching everything I knew about outer beauty, my inner self-worth was not very strong. I was inspiring people with my passionate personality and my presentation, along with a deep desire to make others comfortable. My quest was to make people feel love, by giving them what I thought they needed to feel good. I didn't realize at the time that when people met me I sometimes brought out their insecurities. My intuition told me that people were sometimes uncomfortable with me. I didn't really understand the dance I was doing then, but as soon as someone "shut down," I would try harder to make them feel good about themselves, feel comfortable. This is when I became inauthentic.

I wanted everyone to feel love, so I gave mine away. It was very exhausting. I wanted love so badly that I loved everyone to get it. I realize now that I wasn't letting people feel their own emotions and my behavior was distracting me from feeling mine. To give love to feel love, was the only way I knew. When people were uncomfortable with themselves, I didn't want to feel my darkness, so I filled them up with my light. I was always trying to be the good little girl for love and as I grew up, I became detached and disconnected … because I didn't want to own my untruth and pain.

When I could no longer live with my robot-like personality, I blamed it all on my first husband and left. I realize now that it takes two to break up a relationship. We both had issues and we had lost the communication and intimacy we once had. I can see now that he was the perfect partner for me at the time. His personality enabled me to feel a lot of the darkness that was already in me. Now that I have taken responsibility for myself, I respect and love him. He is a good man and the perfect father for our daughters. I am very grateful that he is in our lives for the many lessons we have all learned. I chose to leave him to find a safe place *in me* to grow.

In the next stage of my life I saw more of the world and began to climb the corporate ladder. I discovered a lot about myself and my fears, about other people and their fears, and from there I connected with the next stage of my life's purpose: ***To inspire others to believe in themselves.***

I am a triplet and my eyes were opened to an opportunity when my identical sister, Frannie, became very ill with environmental sensitivities that caused toxic reactions. I was inspired to develop a unique product line that was not only healthy but also fashionable and on the leading edge of the skincare industry. As CEO and President, and with a talented partner, Charlotte Whaley (Vice-President) and team, we founded and developed a direct-sales company that expanded into the international market, selling skincare, cosmetics and nutritional products. With its remarkable corporate infrastructure, this professional experience gave me the opportunity to build leadership and inspire and motivate others to find personal and professional growth.

The company was called Goldlinx. We started it in Canada with 20 distributors and eventually developed a network of thousands. Taking the company public and then expanding across the United States was an unforgettable experience—years of meeting new people, sharing a vision with them by believing in their self-worth, teaching thousands of people how to embrace their fears, to go outside their comfort zones and share an experience. I taught leaders across the country to inspire groups of people, one person at a time, by being their own best example of feeling good, looking good and taking care of themselves … mind, body and spirit. **To lead by example.**

This journey created opportunities for intense personal growth, and gave me the experience and knowledge to communicate to others the delicate balance between inner and outer attractiveness. I'm not talking about beauty. I'm talking about the fact that when we are connected to our self-worth, we are attractive, we have strength, we have confidence and it shows. We not only look good but we "feel" good to others. They can feel comfortable because we are comfortable.

Outer confidence can give us courage, but we should not mistake it for inner confidence or a sense of self-worth. Developing an inner confidence will support our outer confidence. The journey to our authentic self is like any intimate relationship … it requires truth and commitment.

In the following chapters, I will share daily formulas that I have learned for myself. This way of living has brought my clients and me personal peace and professional success. To have a meaningful relationship with myself and with others, and to realize my life's purpose is woven into everything I do

One evening when I was to facilitate a workshop, I observed people as they came in. They were saying things like: "Don't I know you? You look familiar. How have you been?" I found myself surrounded by people I had never met, yet I was comfortable with them and they were all saying the same things to each other. It felt like we had all known each other for a long time.

I started the seminar by saying we all recognize each other because we have all been to HELL and back and we have met before in this place. We are all the same because we want the same things; what makes us different is our behavior and misbehavior. Each of us has in some way manifested the HELL that is within our experiences and relationships. The packages may be different but the pain and fear are the same. Some of my HELL was dressed up in illness, namely heart problems and cancer, two failed marriages, and a near-death experience when I lost my business. At the same time, my youngest daughter decided it was time to live with her Daddy. The details are not really important—in fact, they can be a distraction—unless you need them to get to your feelings, such as grief, anger, fear, loneliness, and lack of self-worth. Feeling is what is important and personal growth is the result. What is your HELL ... your *misery*, and what do you want to do with it? We have all been there and that is why we recognize each other.

Each journey is individual. Judging ourselves or others is saying that we or they are not perfect. Judging our experience is saying that it is not the perfect experience to help us know what we feel. And this leads us nowhere. In order for me to make progress in my life and take action, I need to embrace my feelings—the ones that keep me stuck in one place and those that make me feel uncomfortable. I had to create tools to help me get through the day so that I could experience my life to the fullest.

All of the books that inspired me made me feel good. I needed to find ways to be happy even when things were awful. I wanted to take action when I was stuck and not be distracted by details. I needed something simple … an easy way to bring myself back to balance … to my center. I was not afraid of pain—in fact, I seemed to be good at attracting painful experiences. I wanted to find the magic in me but I didn't have a good enough memory to remember "the 25 easy ways to success." I just wanted something simple.

LOVE AND PEACE ARE
COMFORTABLE AND ANYTHING
ELSE IS UNCOMFORTABLE AND
IS USUALLY BASED IN

FEAR

— ❤ —

I realized one day that I was always going back to the same things to feel good about myself, to feel love, to feel comfortable, to feel peace. I saw that I had actually developed my own formulas and I discovered that I had created a connection between my emotions and my inner voice, a relationship that never misguided me. I started sharing these formulas with others and found that they worked. I would like to share these formulas with you so that you can experience your day connected to yourself. This connection with yourself will draw people to you, and allow you to inspire them to feel safe to be all that they are. They will remember you because, with you, they have remembered who they are ... To leave behind an unforgettable presence and experience.

— ❤ —

I want you to feel good in your skin and in your life, to love and appreciate the person you are. Rise to your true potential knowing that everything you need is within you. You might be in a place in your life where you don't want to wear your "self" any longer ... you may be tired and want to change **your** dance step. You may be ready for a very important committed relationship with yourself. As with any new relationship, it's time to get to know YOU, *to Look Inside To Find Yourself.*

CHAPTER ONE

LOOK Inside to Find Yourself

Sometimes in our lives we reach rock bottom. We experience what we call HELL. For each of us it's dressed up differently, but for all of us it is dark, tough and devastating. This HELL can be our awakening. Some people call it a breakdown; I believe it is a breakthrough.

This was the sequence of my HELL over three months!

- My second marriage failed
- My business failed
- My daughter left me to live with her Dad
- My health failed (Heart and Cancer)
- My financial security was gone

THIS IS WHAT I FELT
FEAR
    ANGER
        LONELINESS
            BLAME—LACK OF SELF-WORTH

WHO WAS I?

        I WAS A TERRIBLE MOTHER
        I WAS AN UNDESIRABLE WOMAN
        I WAS A FAILURE

I WAS BROKEN

IT WAS LIKE FALLING OFF A BRIDGE

INTO DARKNESS

FALLING OUT OF MY MIND
LOSING EVERYTHING
HATING MYSELF

I WENT INTO THE CLOSET IN MY ROOM. I
CLOSED THE DOOR, CURLED UP IN A BALL
IN THE CORNER

AND WEPT.
I CRIED
FROM THE DEPTHS OF MY BEING
    FOR HOURS.

FINALLY, I SURRENDERED …
I CHOSE TO LIVE.

I decided not to believe in fear any longer because I
realized I had created all my fears.

FEAR STOPS EVERYTHING—
IT CAN BE OUR DISEASE.

I now see how these events changed me. My barriers
were all being shattered. From this place in HELL, I
started to rebuild my own foundation, my belief, my
faith.

**I faced all my greatest fears … I became *humble*.
I STOPPED wearing my old behaviors.**

I THEN STARTED MY JOURNEY
        BACK TO SELF, TO MY HEART

I BEGAN TO REMEMBER WHO I REALLY
WAS. I GAVE MYSELF PERMISSION TO BE
HEALTHY IN EVERY PART OF MY LIFE …
MY MIND, MY BODY, MY SPIRIT.

Self-Worth

It appeared I always attracted relationships in my life with people who were controlling or manipulating. I was afraid to stand up for myself or even to talk about what didn't feel good. What was I so afraid of? Why couldn't I believe in myself at this moment of withdrawal? I know now that my connection to my own self-worth required emotional work on many levels to bring back my confidence in myself. I felt so powerless.

Lauren, my youngest daughter, was home with me for the weekend. I had gone out for a bike ride and was suddenly overwhelmed by all of the burdens in my life. All the challenges I faced were suddenly too huge for me, too heavy. I was afraid and I felt so misused and abused by the people and experiences in my life. I started to remember another time in my life when I had felt this very same way. I felt small, ashamed and unloved. As these emotions surged through my body, I lost control of the bike and fell to the ground. I had braced myself as well as I could, but my eye hit a sharp rock. I got back on my bike but all the way home, people looked at me with such shock that I knew I must be bleeding.

When I got home, I looked in the mirror and saw the damage. Blood was running down my face and my eye was swelling up. It didn't hurt but I felt the emotional pain with my whole body. As I lay on the couch with some ice on my eye, I visualized a familiar feeling, a past experience.

When I was about nine years old in the fourth grade, I had a fantastic young male teacher. He was just out of Teachers' College, in his first year teaching. All of the girls had a crush on him, including me. He was handsome and he was kind. We loved school because he made it great. Math was not one of my favorite classes, but it taught me one of my toughest lessons. We had a math test and the teacher announced that he was going to hand out the grades from the highest mark to the lowest mark and that we were to come to the front and get our paper. I knew I hadn't done very well. I rehearsed the walk from the back of the class to the front each time one of my classmates took the walk. He started at 85 … he was now at 40 and I was still sitting. My knees started to shake, my heart was pounding, my palms were sweaty … it was like a nightmare as the last mark, 24, was called and my name, "Colleen," was announced to the whole world. With each step I was crushed. All eyes witnessed my embarrassment, each of my classmates relieved that it wasn't them. I heard the laughter in the distance but the worst part was when I looked at my teacher … how could he do this to ME!!

I FELT SO small
MY SELF-WORTH WAS SHATTERED
I HELD BACK THE TEARS
I DIDN'T WANT TO LOOK LIKE A BABY
MY HEART WAS BROKEN
I WAS THE DUMBEST ONE IN THE CLASS
I COULDN'T BREATHE

After school I went to Brownies (a young Girl Guide program). I was like a robot as I took my position in the circle and within minutes my anxiety drove me into the cloakroom where I found my jacket. Running out of the school, I started pulling up the zipper of my jacket without even knowing what I was doing. I was in such emotional pain. I pulled the zipper up so fast that it got caught on my throat and I couldn't move my neck as I ran home, blood running down the front of me. When I got home, my mother took me in her arms and carefully eased the zipper down, consoling me in my pain.

As I lay on the couch nursing my eye, the memory of this experience flowed through my body. I had been publicly humiliated by my teacher. I couldn't look at him or my classmates for a long time without feeling stupid. I knew that my parents loved us unconditionally and always supported us but they never confronted the teacher or school board because it just wasn't done in those days. I never spoke about it again to anyone. I had to put the whole experience out of my mind.

I realized that it was no accident that I was facing these feelings again in my life. The fall and the blood were a reminder that I had not healed. The experience had badly damaged my self-worth.

As it happened, I had recently received a birthday card from this same teacher. He had remained on the sidelines in my life and we periodically kept in touch. His phone number was on the card and I thought, "better late than never." I made the call and I took my grade four teacher back thirty years to what, for me, had been a life-altering experience. He did not even remember it, but he showed great compassion. He listened while I shared with him how awful, humiliated and stupid I had felt at the time. He felt badly but I told him it was not my intention to blame him for my feelings, only to tell him how inappropriate his behavior had been. I had allowed this experience to convince me that I was not good enough and it was a gift that I was finally able to tell him how bad I had felt. I told him that I had a pattern in my life of allowing men to control and manipulate me and my sense of self-worth. This was my lesson and by standing up to him so many years later, I was able to heal myself. It was wonderful! He represented all the people in my life that had abused or misused me. By standing up for myself I felt a new sense of inner belief and strength.

That evening, as I tucked my daughter Lauren into bed, I knew something was bothering her. Lauren was nine years old and very bright. She told me that her teacher, her first male teacher, (does this sound familiar?) embarrassed her at school and displayed something she had done at the front of the class. I heard her story and when I asked her what she did about it, I realized, as she told me, that her self-worth was strong. After class, Lauren went to her teacher and told him that what he had done did not make her feel good and she asked him to take her paper down. He apologized to her and took it down. I held my precious Lauren and told her how proud I was of her. I then told her what I had just accomplished with my grade four teacher, even though it was thirty years later. We rejoiced in what we had both done, feeling strong and satisfied that night. The timing of our experiences showed me the mystery of our souls' evolution and the power of our connection with our children.

I FELT THE M Y S T E R Y

- Why did I fall today?

- Why did it trigger the memory?

- I saw myself as small.

- My self-worth was devastated.

- Why did my grade four teacher reappear in my life … thirty years later?

- My daughter was confirmation of the healing.

- The emotional release I embraced was so healing.

- I brought my past to the present and healed one level of my self-worth.

Be Awake

It is not just being present in the moment and going with the flow of life that will take us gently to the next moment. It is about seeing and hearing what is really going on; not to deny ourselves one instance of truth. To be awake to what we see for ourselves and what others say to us. In this instant of each experience know that we have not denied ourselves anything.

We give up so much for another's belief or perception. We deny ourselves of truth for fear of not being loved by another, and with this experience we deny our own love.

We disregard our own feelings for another's fear. We shut down our own beautiful light to feel our lack of power of source when another takes ours for their own.

We dress down because we are in fear of being noticed. We dress down to blend in with the darkness of fear. Take off the cloak of judgment and resentment, this heaviness stops us from feeling the freedom of our self-worth.

Dance with your softness and allow your goddess and god-self to live fully.

We have the balance of male and female energy within when we live honoring ourselves in each moment. We are then open to see others in the same Light.

Surround yourself with this balanced energy to be a constant reminder of who you are. Allow the disconnection of love and peace outside of us to be the light switch for each of us, so that we are not afraid to go inside and feel our own darkness.

Be awake in your life with each relationship, with each experience.

Colleen Hoffman Smith

Self-Discovery

Let's start by being truthful with ourselves. The journey of self-discovery begins with some intimate questions. Am I happy? Do I have peace in my life? Do I like who I am? Do I like to be with myself in the quiet moments? Do I create quiet moments to be with myself? What makes me happy? What do I want?

There is nothing outside of ourselves that will make us truly happy until we feel joy, peace and love within. Let's be realistic and find out who we are, not who we think we should be, or the person others think we are. Our own belief system should be true to self. There is so much in our life that distracts us from feeling ourselves and most of these distractions are driven by fear. Fear of not being good enough or not being accepted, of not being loved. Are you exhausted because you're making everyone else feel love? Are you tired of being nice, fixing everyone else, making everyone else comfortable? Can you take all that energy and give it to yourself?

Give yourself permission *not* to give anyone your love, your pain or your anger. From this day forward commit to living in the present, connected with your self-worth. Let everyone learn how to find their own love inside. If you give everyone your love, in order to make them comfortable, what's left for you? You could be limiting other people's growth because they always need your love and presence to feel good. They can't tap into themselves. They always need someone else to fill them up.

It's time for you to learn to hold on to your own light and love—in every experience, with every person. It's time for you to take responsibility for every emotion and own it, and to find your way back TO YOU. Be authentic and let everyone else choose if they want to enjoy you, be like you or be inspired by you.

We must look at our behavior and be truthful about how we react in every experience. There are a few changes we must commit to in order to be free to alter our lives on so many levels. I found that life became easier when I started to take responsibility for everything. It's easy to take responsibility for success and the wonderful experiences, but what about the tough lessons, the dark experiences? We're all the same, with the same issues. What makes us different is our behavior or our misbehavior. Take Responsibility for every opportunity that will teach us more about who we are.

TAKING RESPONSIBILITY FOR
EVERYTHING
WE ARE FEELING.

THIS IS HUGE.

Everything happening outside of us can lead us to our own feelings. Whatever the experience might be that makes us feel bad, the feelings are still ours.

WE MUST TAKE RESPONSIBILITY FOR ...
OUR EMOTIONS ... WHAT WE FEEL ...

The details, the person,
the experience is the gift that
allows us to embrace our feelings ...
whether they are good or bad.

THOSE FEELINGS ARE OURS TO OWN.

Have you ever been faced with the same experience over and over again, each experience dressed in a different package, yet with the same emotions? The truth is, you will always attract this kind of experience and the people who take you to this same emotional place—abandonment, fear, lack of self-worth, or anger—until you recognize that a pattern has been developing since you were a child, attracting the same result ... or emotions.

Let me take you back to when you were a child—to when you were "programmed." Childhood was when we learned all of our behaviors and when we stopped responding with the truth of our emotions. This is when we learned to be good little boys and girls in order to get love. We learned to be dancing bears to get attention and because being scolded didn't feel good, we went looking for love outside of ourselves.

Sometime in our very young life, we were bundles of love, happy with everything and everyone. Life was magical as we discovered the world around us. But then one day we didn't feel love from one or both of our parents. They may have been there physically, but emotionally they may have been unavailable at times. Our fathers were working hard to provide for the family, perhaps not loving themselves or not knowing how to be present—possibly because they were never taught that these things had to come from within. Our mothers, knowing only how to be a caregiver to others, may not have felt the love inside themselves. Perhaps they had never been taught to love themselves from within.

Put yourself in their place ... you are so busy with work, with so many things on your mind. When your children come to you for attention, how present are you? We all give off energy and we can feel when someone comes into our space bringing anger or joy. We can feel another's energy when they are in love or in hate. We can be in a wonderful mood, but if someone comes into the room and they are withdrawn, we feel uncomfortable.

As children, we were very sensitive to mood changes. If there were issues, problems, fears, or hidden anger around us, we felt it. We would feel uncomfortable and unloved. That's why communication, intimacy and truth are so important, especially with our children ... we all have these feelings. If our parents were in a bad mood or if they were facing problems, how different things might have been if they only could have said to us, "This has nothing to do with how much we love you." Maybe we wouldn't have jumped to conclusions or made assumptions.

Perhaps we also experienced "projection" when a parent who wasn't taking care of his or her own emotions took it out on the children. How unfair that is!

When we were very young and were scolded, we could feel our parents' anger, or we felt their own disconnection from their true self. That might have been when we started the journey to look for love outside ourselves. We sought to become good little girls and boys in our quest for love, and this behavior became conditioned in us. We are loved and rewarded when we perform well and are punished when we misbehave. We look for love in other people and in things outside ourselves. Each experience points to our own lack of self-love. I did the same thing to my children because I learned it from my parents and they learned it from theirs and so on and so on. It only stops when someone finally finds his or her way back to self.

Some experiences in life lead us back inside—pain, loneliness, abandonment, fear, anger, disappointment. These feelings force us to make a choice to either go within and feel, or to numb ourselves with distractions. Everything is inside us … the love, the peace, the happiness, the joy, the wisdom, the strength.

Childhood abuses are never appropriate. People responsible for this sort of dysfunctional behavior are usually disconnected from themselves and this is very sad. Try not to blame your issues and emotional blocks on these past experiences. Blame can also distract us away from feelings. It can distract us from our healing and can be an excuse for not taking responsibility for our present behavior.

Try to move on, beyond your past by bringing your past to the present and by not blaming others or your experiences. Do this by unplugging from your past. But first take responsibility for your emotions, whatever the experience, and feel and embrace those emotions in order to forgive and let the experience go. It will be a challenge until you can feel things fully, and then it becomes an opportunity for growth.

Feel

**WHATEVER THE MEMORY,
THE DETAILS CAN HELP US**

Feel

IT IS ABOUT THE FEELINGS WE SHOVED AWAY

Our quest is to find our way back to self-love. The formulas coming up will assist you in the process of letting go of the past and living in the present. Unresolved feelings always flare up when we least expect them.

B L A M E IS

A VERY FAMILIAR REACTION
TO A BAD EXPERIENCE.

TO **BLAME**

THE OTHER PERSON OR THE EXPERIENCE

IS FORGETTING THAT THE EXPERIENCE

IS A **G I F T** TO TAKE US BACK TO

OUR SELF OR OUR

FEELINGS.

B L A M E

KEEPS US STUCK AND *PLUGGED INTO* PEOPLE
AND EXPERIENCES.

BLAME IS DEFINITELY THE BY-PRODUCT OF *NOT* TAKING RESPONSIBILITY.

We can start by not blaming our parents for our problems. Now that we are adults we need to accept that our parents were dealing with their own pain and survival; they did their best with what they knew, with their own childhood and upbringing. That doesn't mean that any emotional or physical abuse is acceptable, because it's not! But what's done is done, so let's unplug and disconnect from the pain by feeling it … and then find our way back to self-love. We may or may not heal our wounds fully, but by feeling, we can find our way to forgiveness and then we can change our reactions and misbehavior.

It isn't up to anyone to give us love. It's up to us to be the love and to know that it is within us. Take the example of the mother or father who gives everything to the child, filling the child up completely, believing that the child will return the love. This child usually becomes an emotional invalid because he or she has no frame of reference for how to find the love for him/herself inside. It's impossible for them to ever feel happy unless someone is giving everything to them. Many only children experience having everything done for them, but life isn't like that. In my practice I have witnessed many sad stories because the parents gave and gave to their children. These parents were exhausted, while the children learned that there is never enough to fill them up or keep them happy.

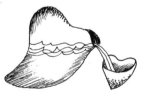

In families that have many children, the youngest gets a lot of attention from the siblings and gets filled up, but many of the others find it lonely unless they are able to reach inside. It all depends on the individual and the example set by the elders. If the parents are present and taking care of their own feelings and sharing and communicating, the process could be the inspiration for love within a family.

Forgiveness allows us to be free of past pain and unfinished business.

To forgive the experience or the other person for their weakness or lack of self-love gives us peace and strength.

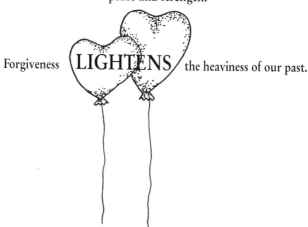

Forgiveness LIGHTENS the heaviness of our past.

Carolyn Myss, author and teacher, teaches us to unplug from the other person or experience.
To forgive allows us to move on, not to be pulled back to being stuck in the past.

FORGIVE

ANYONE IN YOUR LIFE THAT YOU HAVE ANY ANGER OR ISSUES WITH. YOU CAN THEN BEGIN TO REPROGRAM YOUR HABITS, YOUR BEHAVIOR, AND YOUR REACTIONS, AND

LIVE TO BE YOURSELF.

But first you must TAKE RESPONSIBILITY
for how the experience makes you feel, and

FEEL!

As a new mom with my first child, Lindsay, I was definitely having the outer body experience. Not knowing how to love myself, how could I show her love? I did so in the only way I knew, as my mother did for me. I was like a robot, loving her from a very disconnected place. I had my own business, my modeling school. I was busy making everyone happy and not being present in my own self.

Lindsay had her own way of getting our attention. At three weeks old, she stopped breathing and began her first 18 months of life on an apnea monitor. Suffering from apnea, she would stop breathing up to 40 times per day. Night was the worst time. The monitor alarm would bring us running to her immediately. We were so lucky she survived, because many parents are not so fortunate and lose their child to SIDS (Sudden Infant Death Syndrome). Our attention allowed her to feel safe whenever she stopped breathing and we would come running and shake her to remind her to breathe. Sometimes I wonder if she was trying to remind us to breathe and be present, to connect not only with her but with ourselves as well.

Lindsay started looking for love and attention at a very young age. She had a mother and father who were disconnected from their own self-love and self-worth, who were on the same journey looking for love outside of themselves. Lindsay grew to her teenage years experiencing the divorce of her parents, facing a lot of fear and feeling a lot of anger. She blamed me, her father, and the world for her pain. At the time of my greatest darkness, when her sister Lauren decided to live with her father, Lindsay's own darkness mirrored mine. This was painful for me and I started to live differently, taking responsibility. I had forgiven my past relationships. I was no longer blaming anyone or any experiences.

During my own time of self-discovery and change, Lindsay and I had our time of healing. I began to love her from my connected self. Lindsay started to feel my real love. She felt safe with me. As I remembered who I was, she started to see herself. A few years of healing and intimate communication led to a wonderful breakthrough. Lindsay, at 20 years old, forgave me and her father and started to take responsibility for her life. I could see the change in Lindsay, the opening up, and the way she shared her experiences. I felt her difference. I felt her peace. She had connected with her source of love and strength inside and was free to attract experiences that would be created from her abundant self-worth connection and not from her fear. Lindsay is manifesting a beautiful life and I enjoy watching her dance each day with passion. I am so proud of the woman she is.

Now I invite you to **take responsibility** for everything, the good and the bad. Stop **blaming** everyone and every experience for your unhappiness and **forgive** all that has brought you to this place inside yourself. Look in the mirror and see yourself. Are you healthy looking? Do you feel healthy? Be truthful and take the gifts God has given you and love them. See your physical self and if you do not see yourself as healthy and looking the best you can, change your lifestyle to include physical fitness, wellness and an inner workout practice. I will share my inner workout plan in the next chapter. How you eat, sleep and exercise is so important. I encourage you to read Harvey Diamond's books *Fit for Life* and *Fit for Life not Fat for Life*. Harvey has inspired me for 20 years in taking responsibility for my healthy diet. His program is life changing and is key for well-being. Only you can do this for yourself. Look in the mirror and feel. Look into your eyes and allow your soul to speak to you. Be intimate with yourself by being truthful. Falling in love with yourself is the ultimate relationship.

Before I went to my HELL, this is what I saw in the mirror: My physical shell was fashionably dressed and looked great. My image was very put together; makeup fabulous, hair in the latest style, nails manicured. I had taught myself how to take care of my outer package. Physically, I was always well groomed, ate in a healthy way and exercised daily. When I went out, I always looked good. I had confidence in that. It was my self-worth that was lost. I hated to be alone so I was always busy.

When I looked into my eyes,

I WAS S A D

I HAD A LOT OF A N G E R

(I HID MY ANGER BEHIND MY SMILE AND CHATTER)

I SMILED WITH MY LIPS NOT WITH MY HEART

MY EYES HAD NO TWINKLE—THEY WERE GLASSY

I WAS PRETENDING

I DID WHAT PEOPLE THOUGHT I SHOULD DO

MY HEART FELT **DEAD**

I WAS AFRAID AND **UNCeRtAiN.**

I CONTROLLED EVERYTHING TO GET LOVE

I WASN'T SURE IF I EVER REALLY FELT LOVE

INSIDE –

I SPENT MY DAYS MAKING EVERYONE ELSE

FEEL GOOD

I WAS *E X H A U S T E D*

**I LONGED TO REST. I WANTED PEACE.
I WAS ALWAYS SEARCHING FOR SOMEONE TO
MAKE ME FEEL LOVE,
TO FEEL GOOD.**

Self-discovery embraces our own truth about what makes us happy. When we remove judgment and blame and take responsibility for our life, we can find peace and love inside us.

CHAPTER TWO

LIVE To Be Yourself

Three formulas to keep you authentic and attractive are:

> **Formula 1 — The Inner Relationship**
> **Formula 2 — The Inner Workout**
> **Formula 3 — The Inner Peace**

Live Authentic and Attractive

We spend a lot of time not being truthful, doing things for others because we think we have to. We may resent or even hate our days, our work, and our life. We may even walk around all day pretending that we are great and that life is wonderful. Or we may walk around all day wearing our unhappiness, not really feeling any joy at all. Maybe we're stuck in a routine because it's familiar, accepting it all or begrudging it all. We may think we're hiding our emotions from the world, but we're not. If we're closed and quiet, people can feel it and if we're smiling and it's fake, people can feel that, too. If we walk around projecting our anger and letting everyone have it, people will feel it.

Which of these types of people are we comfortable with? If we are truthful, *none of them*! The person who has taken responsibility for their own emotions and has felt them in a healthy way has a chance to find peace and feel peaceful and project peace. We are comfortable with this type of person because they are more comfortable with themselves. The first step to living authentically is being in touch with your emotions. If we don't deal with our emotions inside, if we don't take care of them or own them,

THEY LEAK OUT

Our energy or behavior will tell the truth and create an experience that is not attractive or appealing. The phrase "I cannot tell a lie" should be "I might be able to tell a lie but my energy, behavior or personality will tell the truth." We can always be felt by others, especially if they are present and in touch with their own feelings. We can pretend, but our unfelt emotions, if not taken care of, will show on us. *Stop faking it.* People can feel you.

YOU CAN CHANGE THE ENERGY OF A WHOLE ROOM

From this "pretending" existence, we create our future. I want to teach you to create your future from peace and a place inside that has no fear, that place beyond the uncomfortable where all your answers are:

THIS IS PEACE

Let's get attractive by being authentic. Start by being truthful with yourself and spending time with your feelings, your emotions. This is the most important part of the practice, a practice I would like you to incorporate into your life. There is a body within us— our emotional body. Start slowly and eventually you can be living every minute of the day in touch with yourself and your feelings, instead of letting your emotions run your life. You will eventually be able to

LIVE TO BE YOURSELF.

Connecting with Our Emotional Body

How can we walk into our day, our lives, any room, any experience, personal or professional, without taking care of our own emotions?

Let me give you a formula that will help you:

- ❤ Understand how your emotions influence your behavior.

- ❤ To connect and own your emotions and then feel and heal them.

- ❤ Recognize the path of connection to your own strength and self-worth.

- ❤ Create healthy relationships with yourself and others.

Through this process, you can live authentically, so that others will find you attractive. You can then feel safe to be all that you are with confidence, just by knowing and appreciating your self-worth.

We all have wounds we carry from our childhood. It is in these wounds that our lack of self-worth lies, how we truly see ourselves and how we think others see us.

We are so hard on ourselves; we judge constantly and we self-sabotage our experiences because of our lack of self-love. The place within, where our emotions sit and await our attention, feels like a separate part of us. Our mind and thoughts keep us occupied, and our emotions and feelings keep us distracted. Our mind tries to figure it out and our emotional body keeps trying to get our attention. Our emotions are a passage leading inside to our feelings.

We can ignore our emotions but they will eventually become so powerful that they will attract experiences that force us to feel. If we are depressed, we will attract experiences that are going to make us more depressed. If we don't respect ourselves, we will attract people who don't respect us. If we have self-worth issues, we will attract experiences and people that make us feel unworthy. If we are afraid of loss, we will lose. If we can't be alone, or fear being alone, we will attract a lonely life.

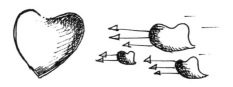

I was afraid of a lot of things and I attracted all my fears. I lived on a merry-go-round and shoved aside all of my emotions. This created illness and loss. Each experience that was uncomfortable forced me to look within.

You don't have to ignore your emotional body any longer.

Moving beyond the details that filled my mind in order to create a compatible relationship with my feelings was difficult. When I meditated, I would usually get distracted by details or fall asleep. I needed a way to connect with my present feelings and I found a simple way to go there and stay there—a place where I went on a little journey. I realized that when I was a little girl, I learned to suppress my feelings because I wanted to be good and to be loved. So when I felt stuff like anger or fear, loneliness or sadness, I covered it up and pretended everything was great. That's where I went off-track and became inauthentic. That's also where I learned to run from my emotions and find someone or something to make me feel comfortable. The essential tool I needed to connect with my emotions had to hold my interest. So I started to "meet" myself when I was a little girl. This connection to my inner relationship was awesome!

The Inner Relationship

Connecting with your Emotional Body.

This tool can be used to find our way back inside—to that place where we need to feel to heal. This is a formula that can be the foundation of your daily practice. This process can free you from the prison of your mind and move you out of the details and chatter, into the connection within.

Close your eyes and concentrate on your breathing. Soft music may help you relax the first time. Put your hand on your solar plexus (above the stomach just below the rib cage).

This is the place where your emotions live. I like to visualize this place as a bridge between my world and "her" world (me, when I was a little child).

Start to walk on the bridge and feel the paradise around you, things that make you feel peaceful—water, sand, flowers, birds, the sky, the forest—whatever makes you feel good.

As you are walking, see yourself as a child walking towards you. Feel the child starting to run towards you. Feel the excitement in your own body as the child comes to you. Your inner child may even jump into your arms. Hold your child in your arms, creating a safe place for your child to be. Feel your love for this child, and feel the heart connection. If, when your child comes to you,

you dislike the child or are repelled (or even feel hate for the child), stay with your child and feel what you are feeling. Were you a wimp when you were a child? Were you a bully? Whatever it is, own it, but don't leave. This is what we (or everyone) did before—we abandoned the child. Create a safe place here by remembering the innocent child and find your way back to love if you can. Tell your child that you will now be the parent and that you will never abandon him/her again. Feel the commitment to the relationship and promise to visit as much as possible.

When you do this, you don't need anyone in your life to take care of you or make you feel better. It's entirely up to you to parent your inner child—you, when you were young—to take care of your own emotions. If you observe people and how they behave and misbehave, it usually looks like a large playground full of children, blaming and judging, hurting and manipulating, to get love. By acknowledging this place in us and by putting the symbol of our own child inside, we can easily go back there to feel what our emotions are up to.

— ❤ —

If you commit to this relationship, the meditation provides an opportunity for you to know yourself and live more in the present. Any emotion other than peace, joy and love is uncomfortable because our emotional body is letting us know that it needs attention. Our symbol for our emotions can be our inner child, *us when we were children.* This is an easy way to have an ongoing relationship with our emotions, our feelings. Try this tool to see if you become more present and a lot more peaceful.

Inner Relationship Summary

❤ Formula 1 is the connection to your emotional body!

❤ To be aware when you shift from comfortable to uncomfortable.

❤ To be with any emotion and to know when you are not connected to your own source of love.

❤ Formula 1 takes you inside to this place of connection—to be committed to feel.

❤ This relationship is the connection to the fountain of youth—PEACE.

The Inner Workout

*Part I • Staying emotionally
fit—Getting rid of the heaviness*

Take responsibility for experiences other than success.
We must practice each day to be in touch with
what we are feeling. What makes us feel
uncomfortable? Anything other than
peace is a reaction to our emotional body
that needs to be felt, given attention to
and understood.

A lot of us get up in the morning and feel anxiety,
upset stomach, lack of excitement, butterflies, or nerv-
ousness. We drag ourselves out of bed with heaviness
and fear, and as the morning unfolds, we shove aside
the feeling without even noticing. We think we have
dealt with it or that it is gone. What we have done,
however, is put it away, ignored it and walked into our
day without clearing away the heaviness and the wor-
ries. It can be overwhelming to even attempt to figure
it out.

Feeling it out is what I would like you to try to do.
Take the time to acknowledge your feelings. Get connected each day before you even get up. As we travel
through our days, people and experiences will trigger
us if we have not dealt with our emotional issues. The
details help us get to the emotions, clearing the heaviness, which could be anger, fear, loneliness, or self-

worth issues. Anything that feels uncomfortable triggers us to take action so that we can feel comfortable. It's time to own these feelings and not ignore them.

I was doing a seminar at a fitness center that I called "The Inner Workout." The seminar was all about getting in touch with and getting rid of the heaviness we carry inside. The seminar was mostly on anger and how we suppress it and carry it around, how it can leak out, or how it can be projected when you least expect it. I was just getting comfortable with the group when the receptionist ran in and asked for my help. A woman was very upset and yelling at her. The step class she usually attended had been cancelled and replaced by the seminar. We could all hear this woman screaming.

I excused myself from the group and approached the woman calmly and asked her what she was upset about. She was projecting her anger all over the place! Suddenly the receptionist engaged with the woman and they both started yelling at each other. I separated them and explained to the woman that this seminar had been advertised for two months and I was sorry that she was so upset. I suggested that maybe she would benefit from the seminar, which was about dealing with anger. She wanted no part of it and huffed off. The receptionist then hurried away. When I returned to the seminar, I explained that this had not been staged; however, it was a perfect example of what suppressed anger could do.

After the seminar, I talked to the receptionist, who felt bad about her behavior. I reminded her that she must have had some anger in her that was triggered by the woman's anger because she had reacted to the anger and engaged with the upset woman. I suggested that she could now own the anger that had been ignited, to try to stay centered and calm, and not allow anyone to take their anger out on her. When someone is in such an intense emotional state, don't engage with them.

We have all been on both sides of this fence. Anger is a very toxic ingredient to add to any experience or relationship. Projecting anger is never appropriate. We can get angry and tell someone, but if our own anger is not taken care of, the words will be highly charged. Projection of this kind is abusive. If one person in the situation can remain calm and unaffected, the other person has the choice to remember the peace instead of the anger. This is when we can go to places in us that need to be embraced and owned. If someone is projecting anger and we are not triggered by it, we are able to set boundaries and speak from a strong sense of self-worth.

I later found the unhappy, angry woman on the Stairmaster. I approached her with a big smile, thanking her for being the example for my seminar. She stopped and said, "What do you mean?" I replied: "The seminar was about anger and projecting it on others." I added, "What would you have done at that moment of rage if your son had came out of the playroom and tugged at your sleeve? What would you have done with him? What would your child have felt from you?" In a quiet voice she asked: "What could I have done?" I replied: "You could have owned your anger and not given it to anyone, and maybe come to the seminar. Believe me, the whole experience was perfect for everyone to see. You played your role to show us all a picture of what we can do in our life. So thank you for being a great example for my seminar."

She did come to the evening program and realized that this kind of misbehavior happens a lot in her life. She started to own her anger and by not suppressing it or projecting it, she learned to take care of it.

Going to the bridge and allowing your inner child to have a tantrum by pounding a pillow is a lot safer than projecting your anger onto someone. It releases the anger that you might feel towards them, and then allows you to find your way back to peace.

What Triggers You?

Certain personalities may arouse emotions in us. We could be in a confident, wonderful mood and someone suddenly makes our blood boil, or shuts us down. We have all been wounded by relationships and experiences. We were first wounded when we were children and this is when we learned how to react and behave. That's when we lost our connection to some or all of our self-worth.

This wound has made us judge others and ourselves. We hold on to this wound, carrying it forward into our life. This wound could be because we were physically or emotionally abandoned. This wound could be because we were given everything and didn't learn how to feel good on our own. We could have had an angry parent so we learned to withdraw and not to speak. Lack of self-worth is wrapped around every wound.

IF WE HAVE A LOT OF UNFELT ANGER OR RAGE

WE WILL ATTRACT EXPERIENCES

THAT BRING IT OUT

TO BE

FELT.

If we have abandonment issues, we will attract people in our lives who will emotionally or physically leave. If we are afraid of something, we will attract fearful experiences until we feel safe within ourselves. If we have commitment issues, we will attract people and experiences that can make us feel the lack of commitment. Do you sometimes feel like a bad girl or bad boy? When we were children, we sometimes felt we were a disappointment to our parents or friends. This experience creates a wound of self-doubt. Fear of many things can be huge in us, and each time we feel unsafe, we go to that fear. So, before we can handle the triggers in life, we must discover our wounded self. This place where we feel uncomfortable can also attract discomfort. It is easy to embrace peace, joy and love. It feels great, because it feels comfortable. To focus on our breathing and acknowledge the trigger helps us go inside and own it, and then embrace it, feel it, before we react. We might even feel love but then we might quickly shut it out because love can bring out our sense of unworthiness.

Peace is where our centered confidence and self-worth lives. This is where we feel love and joy. This is God and the connection is everything. It doesn't matter what higher power or religion you believe in, this is where that higher power lives. I am spiritual and I honor all religions. This power is within you—your belief in yourself—trusting that the peace and love are always there. Just as the sun is always there, though sometimes it's hidden by clouds. When we own the feelings that are triggered in us, we can change the dance step. The density of our pain sometimes blocks the way to love. Use this formula as a tool to summon your emotions and clear the way for love and peace to shine through.

If an experience or person triggers our wound, we feel something immediately. The energy, the vibration of the words and the actions of another or an experience can ignite our emotions. When you experience this disconnection, you can quickly put your hand on your heart to remind yourself to get present. The vision of your child will quickly show you. That is why seeing your child or feeling your child can take you where you need to go—inside— instead of abandoning your emotions and reacting to or engaging with someone in an uncomfortable way. Your reaction might be to shut down or to project onto someone else. Instead, go to the relationship inside you and hold your inner child; feel your emotions until you feel peace.

Feel that emotion fully.

When you do the practice and visit your inner child on the bridge each day, you can have a strong, safe relationship with your feelings. You can even go to the bridge and put someone there and practice with his or her energy. The bridge is the safe place to change your behavior, reprogram yourself. The first thing you must do is get any anger, fear, resentment, judgment or blame out of yourself. This is the place to get it out. When you are on the bridge you can instantly feel the energy of the person who really triggers you. And while you are feeling it, get it out. Scream, cry, pound a pillow, have a tantrum—FEEL—just get out the unspoken words and hidden feelings.

Once you release these suppressed emotions, you will have more space for peace and love. When you are in this place inside, you can push away the darkness and pain by feeling it and expressing it in a healthy way. This is a great way to practice getting to that place of peace with people and relationships. The practice helps clear the heavy cloud of hurt, pain, fear, anger and resentment. This inner workout can be incorporated into your life. Instead of reacting, shutting down or projecting, you can keep your cool and be more authentic and much more attractive. You can confront your suppressed emotions here on the bridge instead of projecting them to others. If you lose it, or go insane for a moment, please, please take time to look at your misbehavior. Allowing yourself, your inner hurt child, to feel, makes the experience purposeful. Take responsibility for your own feelings. When you have to address an issue with someone, it doesn't have to be embraced with past resentment.

When you look around and feel the people in your world, you will notice three personalities and types of behavior:

- ♥ The person who is the **victim**— quiet, shut down, withdrawn.

- ♥ The **bully** or **petty tyrant**— aggressive, projecting, controlling.

- ♥ The **peaceful** person— balanced, open, easy to be with.

Which of these people looks and feels attractive to you?

Both victim and bully have conditioned behaviors for self-protection. Both of these behaviors have been worn since childhood. The best time to deal with our issues is when our emotions feel uncomfortable. Shoving them away and ignoring them is not the healthiest way to do it. Problems will definitely arise when we least expect them. As you discover the truth about your emotions and feelings, you will discover who you are, why you attract your life experiences and how to change your life. The behavior we feel more comfortable with is the place of peace. This inner connection can shift every experience into an opportunity for growth. In peace we can find strength, courage and power.

THE CHALLENGE CAN BE THE OPPORTUNITY!

The Inner Workout

Part II
Clearing the Weight

The Triggers in Our Life

Any experience or person that makes us feel uncomfortable has triggered us out of our place of peace and love. This negative reaction has made us feel something and that is a gift—feeling something in us that needs to be owned. The uncomfortable experience, words, personality or even the energy of another person would not bother us in this way if we were centered and connected to our present peace. The uncomfortable experience is waking us up to go to the place inside that needs attention. Instead of blaming these experiences or people, see the beauty of the awakening. The emotions that flare up in us are coming from our past. This moment of feeling is the moment of self-discovery and we have this uncomfortable trigger to thank for bringing our past to the present.

Many people in our life trigger us. Because of this disconnection from ourselves we sometimes touch that fine line between sanity and insanity. We can react when triggered by projecting (being the bully), or shutting down (being the victim).

By taking responsibility for whatever emotions we are feeling and then being free of blame or charge, we can put the experience on the table and speak about it from a centered place.

When I would shut down, I couldn't speak. I was afraid to share my feelings until eventually I would either get sick or become an emotional mess. I know that when I was closed I was feeling a lot inside. When I was shut down, my children, family or friends felt uncomfortable. When someone is shut down or a victim, it can be tiresome for others. I didn't like this behavior in me; it wasn't comfortable. My inner workout took me inside myself, creating the safe place to embrace my hurts and past pains. I became aware of the uncomfortable emotions that shut me down. I saw how my behavioral frame of reference came from my childhood. Shutting down was my protection.

I practiced finding my way back to my own self-worth and love. I didn't want to be afraid anymore. I decided I wanted to change my misbehavior. I took responsibility and realized how preprogrammed I was to shut down and be nice. My behavior enabled others to control and manipulate me, and hurt me. It was my responsibility to change, to get more comfortable with me.

The moment of negative ignition, when we feel uncomfortable, is the time to do the practice.

Put your hand on your heart to remind you to breathe.

Instead of reacting, go to the emotions, own them and embrace them. Go to your breathing to connect with your feelings instead of reacting. This is where you can change your dance step and heal your past programming, by changing your misbehavior. Remember—whatever you are feeling is always about you; it is not about trying to change the other person. The time for our healing is when we own our emotions and experiences. This is when we are connecting to our present feelings and owning them, when we are remembering who we are. The other person then has a chance and a choice whether or not he or she wants to remember who they are. Instead of mirroring each other's fear, anger or blame, you can remember your peace—you don't have to react in a negative way.

So breathe deeply and feel your child inside you and connect with your vulnerability. Allow him or her to feel, creating a safe place. Embrace that child until you feel good. This could take just one breath—to remember.

We usually attract the same experiences over and over again. They might be dressed up differently but our feelings of anger, doubt or fear are the same. Once we surrender to learning a new behavior, take responsibility and feel our self-worth, we no longer have to attract the uncomfortable experiences or people. The uncomfortable experiences may be all around us, but we don't have to be triggered and react to them.

Triggers: Lack of Self-worth... Suppressed Anger

Sandy called me one evening and told me the details of what had been going on recently. She was overwhelmed and very upset. I could feel she was at a breaking point. I could feel her fear. Sandy seemed always to be attracting experiences that were very toxic and violent. Each uncomfortable experience or relationship would give rise to her anger and defenses. She would react by engaging or projecting anger. On several occasions, she lost it and her anger became verbally aggressive and loud. She had come to a crossroad in her life and she just didn't want to fight any longer. She was surrendering her past and she didn't want the struggle. She asked me what she could do to shift her life, because she was so tired.

Sandy had realized that her conditioned behavior and reactions were not the way to her peace and purpose. Like all of us, Sandy had a lot of suppressed anger. I shared with her my belief that we must embrace our own anger and work it out of our body in a healthy way. If we don't take responsibility for our anger, we wear it, or we project it and try to give it to someone else. This anger deep inside can stop us from loving fully and living authentically. Sandy felt that she could be easily triggered, which is why she protected herself so much. She often kept herself closed and wearing her inauthentic mask.

— ❤ —

Sandy's self-worth and belief in herself was always being tested, creating experiences that would make her feel unloved or not good enough. Not feeling safe within, being triggered out of the connection to peace, made Sandy feel unattractive to others. She was tired and experiences were coming fast and furious, forcing her to feel the pain and search inside for answers. She was unhappy and insecure in her job. Management was blocking her growth and passing her by, not respecting her talent, knowledge and expertise. Sandy was constantly having "run-ins" with heads of departments. She had recently bought a house and her investments were crashing. She was losing child support from her ex-husband. She was going deeper into debt and, with job cuts on the horizon, her job was in jeopardy. She was losing control and feeling a lot of pain and fear. SANDY WAS IN HER EMOTIONAL HELL. SHE WAS LOSING CONTROL.

THIS IS THE TIME TO SURRENDER—
THE AWAKENING TO A NEW PLACE INSIDE.
IT IS ALSO OUR CHOICE TO SHIFT OR NOT.
WE CAN GO TO THIS PLACE AS MANY TIMES
AS WE NEED TO IN OUR LIFE. WE HAVE THE
OPPORTUNITY TO CHANGE OUR LIFE IF WE
SURRENDER, TAKE RESPONSIBILITY AND
THEN TAKE ACTION.

Sandy's anger had been resonating in her, attracting these experiences to make her go inside to feel. She had a lot of childhood anger, as we all do, carried and leaking out when least expected. She was constantly being challenged. Sandy learned this dance step in her very feisty relationship with her mother. She never felt good enough in her mother's eyes. She always felt her mother's disappointment and she seldom felt her mother's love. Sandy expressed herself from a deeply wounded place: *My Mother Was Never Proud of Me.*

Sandy cried as she embraced her wounded child inside. Her mother was most likely proud of Sandy but could seldom show her. Some of our mothers didn't know how to love from a place of self-love. It's hard to be intimate with our own love when we are not connected to it. Sandy was afraid that she was creating the same experience with her children. I told her that her mother was a great gift, showing her how not to parent and this supported her choices in life. It was up to Sandy to be proud of herself and not feel that she needed anyone, any experience to make her feel good about herself or feel love. Each person that she was attracting in her life who made her feel not good enough triggered the little girl inside who yearned for her mother's love and approval. *The little girl inside needs to be embraced and not abandoned.* It was necessary for Sandy to realize that it wasn't up to her mother to fill her up with love or confidence; it was already all inside of her to feel and know herself.

When dealing with her own children, it's up to Sandy to love them from a place connected to the love inside, not from a hurt child inside. Each time she is triggered, it is a reminder to be present and feel. Connect to the feelings and shift the perception. Change the idea of unloved to loved, lack of self-worth to self-worth, fear to safety, anger to peace—for yourself. You do this FOR YOU. It's called taking care of yourself.

All of Sandy's experiences were reminders of the child inside not feeling love. This is the time to go to that child and feel her and create a safe place. Don't abandon her now. Allow her to own her feelings, feel them and express them within your safe embrace. And then show her that you still love her.

Sandy saw how she truly had to believe in herself, be proud of herself, and love herself so she would no longer attract experiences that brought her back to the abandoned love. She had connected to the place with her mother and her childhood that she suppressed and held in her body—where she had lost her connection to her self-worth, where she could get in touch with her anger and blame. She started to have a relationship with her little girl inside. She forgave her mom and she realized all of her mom's gifts. Sandy started living differently and realizing her own gifts. She started feeling good about herself. Sandy started to take care of her anger in a healthy way, not wearing it or projecting it. She softened; she connected more with her Goddess self, her inner beauty. She became more attractive, easy to be with. Sandy's life changed because she was remembering who she was. Sandy was more authentic and safe within herself. She didn't have to guard her feelings because she was now taking responsibility and parenting her inner child. She was embracing her emotions. She was inspired and she was inspiring without projecting her negative emotions. The peace she was touching created a happier life.

— ❤ —

A great way to feel the anger and release it is to find yourself a private space and relax into your breathing. Go to the bridge and create a safe place for your inner child. Bring the person or experience to the bridge that is hooking into the anger and feel it come up into your emotional body. Breathe into it and feel it. Allow your child inside to express herself. Pound a pillow if you can. Release the emotion. This could take five minutes or one hour. Don't abandon your inner child. Visualize the bridge and stand in front of the person who is triggering you. Use them, here on the bridge, and talk to them, feel, scream. Do whatever you need to do to feel your pain with this one who is in your life, to show you this part in you. Stand up to the bully, or speak the truth to the one who shuts down from you. As soon as you feel empty of the anger and resentment…see a cord connected to that person…cut the cord…visualize the cord dissolving. At this moment, connect to your own self-love…your inner source of love. Stand in front of this person who you have emotionally let go and feel your own peace and connection to love within. You don't need anything from them, not their love or their pain. Forgive them if you can and feel your own love in your heart. Inspire them as you stand on the bridge, practice here with anyone who triggers you.

The key part of this exercise is to reconnect with your own source of self-love and self-worth…to feel it inside you.

You must not skip this part. This is the way to fill up the space where your self-hatred and anger live. Each time we use the people and experiences in our lives to feel our resentment we can create more space for peace.

Embrace your child once you feel you have released the anger. Relax within the peace of your relationship. Feel the space you have inside where your anger was living by bringing your love to this space. Feel the present moment. Feel the connection to all that you are.

Triggers: Inauthentic Behavior ...
Low Self-worth ...
Shame...
Unresolved issues

George sat across the table from me one day saying that he was really tired of the struggle he was having with a co-worker. Maggie appeared to have a very strong personality and was never fair; she was always playing games. George never felt safe with her and it was important that they have a productive, professional relationship in order for them to work together effectively as a team. As he talked to me about the details, it was apparent to me that his co-worker, Maggie, did not feel safe with George. George was blaming her for the poor relationship and I felt, as he was giving me only his side of it, that there was some hidden, unfinished business standing in the way of their working relationship. I asked George if there was anything from the past that might have caused Maggie to not feel safe with him. He looked at me and said yes. I could see in his eyes that he was touching a part of his past that he had not looked at or felt in a long time. He poured out the experience that he had buried about Maggie. This past experience was unfinished business that he was carrying with him, and it prevented him from being authentic in his life, especially with Maggie at the office.

He talked about when he was new with the organization and he realized that an associate was behaving unethically. He didn't understand the procedure or the position of this associate. George reported the associate, thinking that he was doing the right thing, but later found out that the associate was working under Maggie's direction. Maggie felt betrayed by George. During the process of exploration, Maggie had to take responsibility for the associate's misconduct. Luckily, Maggie and the associate were cleared of any unethical behavior.

I could see the embarrassment and pain George felt about the whole experience. All concerned had felt betrayed. Now Maggie didn't feel safe with George. As well, there were others in the organization who didn't trust George and he had felt it for years. The experience with Maggie had not helped his self-worth. I asked him what he would do now if an associate were misbehaving. He said he would go to Maggie and inform her, giving her the chance to deal with it. He realized that this past experience was unfinished and this place of insecurity within him was because he felt ashamed that he could never be himself with Maggie. She was still hurt and he was hiding from it. It didn't make him feel good about himself and around Maggie he felt powerless. Her anger was always leaking out at him.

As he spoke about the experience, George decided to take responsibility for the existing relationship. A perfect opportunity presented itself a few days later when he met with Maggie. It gave him the chance to bring the past to the present. He apologized for his lack of knowledge at the time and said that he certainly would do things differently today, by taking the matter to her. He felt a lot better afterward and felt more authentic in the relationship. He brought the past to the present with Maggie. Their relationship slowly shifted because George took responsibility and did not blame her anymore. He forgave himself and her for the misbehavior.

George looked at this barrier in his life and shifted it by owning the experience. He realized that the uncomfortable relationship with Maggie was all about him and was triggered by the unresolved experience with her. George is now a lot more comfortable with himself and others in his life. The part of him that was blocked was constantly being triggered because he had not owned the experience and felt it fully. He went to the bridge and he felt the emotions of the past with Maggie. He then felt free of resentments and no longer had to carry these suppressed feelings around, creating experiences that made him feel guilty or like a bad boy. His ego had stopped him from owning the misbehavior and he blamed others to feel better. Now he is free to be himself.

— ❤ —

George went to the bridge between the worlds of the past and present and spent time with the experience and his little boy. He embraced his child and the emotions he was feeling of not being good enough, not being loved, and how he always blamed Maggie for how awful he felt. She, on the other hand, always felt this energy of blame and was never safe with him.

George created a safe place to feel his little boy and then he reconnected with his own source, the place of self-love, peace and self-worth. He then brought Maggie on the bridge and felt his anger at how she treated him. With her on the bridge, he could feel her energy and the loss of his own power and connection. He felt his anger and then went to forgiveness; he felt his own self-love again. With his self-worth and connection to the present, he could now face Maggie with the truth, free of the triggers of the past, bringing the relationship into the present.

**Triggers: Lack of Self-worth ...
               Standing up to the Bully**

Belinda sometimes had trouble looking into my eyes. She would feel agitated or she could not receive love easily. She realized that she would often emotionally leave an experience or a person. We had good sessions together, always dealing with self-worth issues. Belinda was very plugged into her healing process and she constantly took ownership of her uncomfortable experiences, always looking inside to find the answers. But she was attracting a lot of bullies in her life who were causing her to feel bad about herself. The bullies were always there but she was beginning to see more clearly that this was about her. These people were saying or doing hurtful things and she found herself shutting down, leaving, cutting them out of her life or projecting back. These experiences and people were definitely bringing out her anger and her lack of self-worth and love. She was suppressing her real feelings and not being authentic or truthful. This behavior created uncomfortable feelings and because of them she was shutting down her playfulness, her peace. She frowned, her eyes were dark, and there was no joy. Belinda didn't like how she felt and she just wanted to run away from these relationships that were demeaning and abusive. It was time for her to become safe inside and be truthful.

There were four people Belinda felt she had unfinished business with and she took responsibility for her part. She stopped blaming them and she forgave them for their misbehavior. She realized that when they were not feeling good about themselves, they would put her down. Belinda began to realize that the reason she was being triggered was because it awakened the part of her that did not feel good about herself.

Once she connected to her emotions and felt safe, Belinda had an opportunity to talk to each of these people and to stand up to them. She felt safe enough in herself to tell them what she felt about their misbehavior and how she was no longer going to accept it in their relationship. She did not want to be abused or demeaned any longer. This freed her and brought her relationships into the present. She discussed the past relationships and her feelings about them. Without judgment she talked about her feelings and thanked the four people for being in her life to show her the parts of herself she did not love. She used these people to feel her pain and resentment. She stood up to the bullies in her life. On the bridge she contemplated, she visualized, and her experience of truth took her to the depth within herself to feel, as she meditated and reconnected with her own peace and love.

Belinda felt better about herself and felt she could be more authentic with them or anyone with the same abusive energy and behavior. Belinda felt and owned her feelings of not being good enough. The next time anyone said something disrespectful, if she felt hurt or angry, instead of projecting or shutting down, she felt her emotions, remembered who she was, and talked about how she felt. She found that the relationships changed because she changed. She didn't have to attract negative experiences to make her feel bad about herself, because she truly did not. Belinda spoke the truth and was now trying to be more authentic in every relationship.

— ❤ —

The Practice

We can go to the bridge and practice with anyone we are feeling uncomfortable stuff with. Breathe and connect with yourself. See the bridge and walk towards it. Feel aware of the beauty around you, that which brings you to peace (beach, trees, mountains, streams), find your child and create a safe place with the child to embrace their emotions. Remember the love by loving them. Feel connected inside, peaceful and happy—away from the details of the mind. Once you feel safe, bring anyone you need to practice with onto the bridge. Because we are all energy, we can feel them even if they have passed on. You can feel anyone at anytime. Feel whatever emotions come up in you when they are standing in front of you. Be truthful— FEEL. If it's anger, feel it. If it's loneliness, feel it. If it's control and intimidation, feel it. Allow your emotions, your child inside, to feel and speak about it. Tell them what you're feeling. Cry if you feel like it. Hit a pillow and get the anger out if you have to. If you are repelled, feel it. Write about it.

This is the time to embrace the feelings this person or experience brings up in you. Own them, feel them, and then allow the love and your peace to replace the cloud of negativity. Once it is embraced and released, hook onto the suppressed emotions waiting to be felt. This is how we clear the weight inside and create more space to feel lighter. We can practice with anyone, so that when that particular kind of energy is with us, we do not have to react or shut down. We are able to speak without charge, blame, or judgment. It is important to reconnect with your own love once you have let go of all the heavy suppressed feelings.

In a professional setting, when feeling misunderstood or demeaned, take the time to remember who you are and before confronting or reacting, don't assume anything, especially the worst. Table your concerns once you get clarity. Sometimes just by asking for clarity, you are asking the other person to own part of the experience. Then you can talk about your concerns. Try to create some intimacy and communication. If you are too upset, or the other person is, postpone the discussion until later.

The Trigger of Suppressed Anger

I constantly attracted a certain type of person in my life. Male or female, it did not matter. There was always someone in my life I felt uncomfortable with. This type of person usually had a strong, aggressive personality. They would be in my life until I could no longer take it. I would either leave the relationship physically by ending it or, leave the relationship emotionally and shut down. I usually did it with blame or judgment, always saying to myself, "What more can I give to this person? They're never happy. I can never give enough or what I give is never good enough." I would be exhausted by the relationship and have to watch what I said when they were there, or, when they left, I was glad they were gone. This type of relationship made me so uncomfortable I would eventually avoid the person. One day, I finally got it, and this is how I changed my dance step. This is how I stopped attracting this kind of experience in my life.

One day, when I was feeling physically very low with a bad flu, a friend of mine called. This friend had the kind of energy I have just described. I was at the point in our relationship where I was not feeling very good about it. I was so uncomfortable with her and I knew I was not being authentic. At times I was watching every word I said and other times, when I felt safe to be myself, depending on her mood, I might get a tongue-lashing. I was not feeling very comfortable or safe with this relationship. When she was happy and feeling good, we had a great time. But if she was not feeling good, I felt her anger between the words, in her breath.

This particular day I was very sick but we needed to connect about an outing the next day. I told her I was not well and could not talk long. I was going to bed for the day. Sometime during the conversation, I told her I had to go and she blew up at me. I got off the phone feeling a lot of anger. I got into bed and I looked inside to find out what was in me that needed to be owned. How could I change my dance step so that I didn't have to attract this kind of experience any longer?

I went to the bridge and welcomed myself when I was a child. I went into this familiar emotion and I saw myself with my mother, trying to make her feel good, to feel love. I found myself shutting down my feelings and walking on eggshells, trying not to create any discomfort for my mother. I didn't want to feel her anger, the suppressed anger that she was sure she was hiding from us. She too was taught as a child to keep her emotions inside. There had been a lot of anger and lack of love in her home.

I brought to the bridge all the past and present relationships in my life that I had the same experience with. I felt them all one by one and I felt with each of them the experience that made me feel awful. Those people who, throughout my life, had made me feel uncomfortable. I had left them quietly or had blamed them openly. I remembered how they didn't respect me and I kept quiet, how they manipulated me and I shut down, how they controlled my happiness and I allowed them. I felt how I did everything I could to make them feel comfortable, feel love, but it was never enough.

I FELT POWERLESS. I SCREAMED

I CRIED

I STAMPED MY FEET
—I FELT DEEPLY.

I TOLD EACH PERSON HOW I FELT ABOUT
THEIR MISBEHAVIOR.

HOW THEY MADE ME FEEL.

THEY WERE MEAN TO ME.

MY LITTLE GIRL WAS HURT.

I COULD NOT GIVE THEM ENOUGH.

THEY MADE ME FEEL UNSURE
OF MYSELF.

I HIT MY PILLOW UNTIL I COULD NOT CRY
AND SCREAM ANYMORE. I FELL INTO
AN EXHAUSTED STATE.

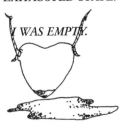

I WAS EMPTY.

I kept feeling this anger and realized that there had always been someone in my life who could bring me to this place. I spent the afternoon holding my child inside. I saw that when I was in this place of disconnection, not feeling my own anger, I stopped the love for myself inside. I abandoned my self-worth. I wanted to feel peace again, so I went to the bridge to find my inner child—me when I was a child. I embraced her, showing her how much I loved her. I didn't want to abandon her. I wanted her to know it was okay to feel all of the emotions that were held in the body over the years. I was not a bad girl and the bridge was a safe place for me to get it out—the anger, sadness and hate that had not been fully felt.

I OWNED THE ANGER.

We all have anger that we have suppressed and I realized that the reason I had attracted these relationships was to feel all of the past anger that I did not want to own. It was easier to blame another for my uncomfortable feelings. I also saw how when someone brought anger or inauthentic behavior (which are suppressed feelings covered up) into my space I would then become inauthentic myself. I would try to make them comfortable instead of expressing myself or telling them I was feeling uncomfortable. I'm sure my inauthentic behavior didn't feel good to them either. So we would both have an uncomfortable experience. I would become guarded because I didn't want their anger to leak out and I would try to fill them up with love. I would become the good little girl.

Now that I felt all my past anger, I was in the present and with a very loving and compassionate heart, I confronted each person on the bridge and forgave them and even thanked them for the gift of showing me my anger. I practiced being the love in front of them, not giving them anything, and I felt peace.

My friend and I had a major healing. I shared with her my experience and said that I was going to change my behavior. I was not afraid of my anger any longer. I created a way to feel it in a healthy practice. I hoped that she could feel me being more authentic when she brought her anger into my space. I acknowledged when I felt uncomfortable instead of trying to make her feel good. I thanked her for being such a great gift in my life, showing me my anger. We embraced and each took responsibility for our misbehavior. Our relationship has continued to grow, finding safety and truthfulness, returning to the love.

Toxic, abusive communication will destroy any relationship. Now that I try my best to return to self-worth when I am abused or someone behaves inappropriately with me, I can be true to self by acknowledging that I don't need or want anyone to project on me. Sometimes we must become a little ruthless and stand up to abusive behavior. Communication and intimacy have different depths depending on the relationship itself. Honoring ourselves by standing up to toxic behavior is important for our self-worth. Honoring all of our sisters and brothers ultimately creates comfortable, important relationships.

I believe everyone's wound is about lack of self-worth and not feeling good about ourselves. This is the foundation of all our painful emotions. When two people feel this wound at the same time, it can ignite powerful responses. In this place, both parties forget who they are and don't feel self-love. They also forget who the other person is. In this place someone must try to take the higher ground, to believe in the vision of the relationship, without blaming the other person, and try to feel the peace. This is the toughest part in a relationship: Changing our dance step and remembering the love.

I did not go back and call each person in my life who triggered my anger, but from then on, I reprogrammed my reactions and behavior and because of my practice, I don't get triggered very often. With working relationships, I just practice being more authentic and clear.

When we can look at each experience and own the part that is ours, we are then free to acknowledge the part of the experience that we do not have to take. By doing this, we show respect for ourselves and don't abuse our worth. Many times, I have felt abused and by going to the person and getting clarity, I realized that they hadn't meant to abuse me. If they did, my tabling the experience and asking for clarity let them know that I was aware of the situation. Whether or not they admitted it, didn't matter—what mattered was that I didn't abuse myself.

There is the experience and the result, and somewhere in the middle,

This awareness can create the shift in self-worth and relationships.

Communicating to someone when triggered

- 💜 First try not to react.

- 💜 Breathe and get centered.

- 💜 If you cannot get back to your feelings quickly or do not have time to connect and feel peace, try saying something like this:

  "I'm feeling your anger. Let's talk later."

  "I'm feeling some anger. Would you like to talk about it?"

  "Is something going on with you?"—or— "How are you?"—or—"Would you like to talk about it?"

  "This is not feeling good right now. What's going on?"

- 💜 Try not to take someone else's anger personally but let them know you feel it. Table it.

- 💜 Create the communication with them either at the moment of trigger or once you have taken care of your own emotions.

- 💜 Eventually, you can get good at standing up for yourself without putting down the other person.

- 💜 See the weakness in them and try not to go to weakness yourself. Be compassionate. The trigger is the gift to feel.

Now I know I'll try hard to change my behavior. When a person with anger enters my space, I put it on the table. I say, "I'm feeling uncomfortable. Can we talk about it?" or, if I feel anger, I take responsibility and embrace it as *my* anger and then, without charge, I share the fact that I feel something is wrong and say, "Would you like to talk about it?" Occasionally I have to take care of my anger in a healthy way. When I start feeling uncomfortable or agitated by experiences or people, I know it's time for me to face my unfelt emotions.

It's amazing how I've healed this dance with others and find that I'm not triggered by another's anger. But when people bring it to me, I acknowledge it. If it's an inappropriate behavior, I do my best to say so, but without anger or charge. We do not have to take it in or project it out. I decided that it was too exhausting to make people feel good, to feel love, and I was not going to be the light for anyone any longer. **I GAVE MYSELF PERMISSION TO *BE* THE LOVE AND NOT *GIVE* THE LOVE.** It is up to each person to take responsibility for his/her own happiness and I am taking care of my own. When I remember who I am, others have a chance to remember who they are.

- *It's a gift to feel what I need to feel.*
- *Be authentic, own your feelings, don't blame others.*
- *You do not have to make anyone comfortable any longer. Take care of your own emotions.*
- *Bring your emotional body to the present. Empty each day by embracing your feelings.*
- *Fill your emptiness with self-love, peace and trust.*

Inner Workout Summary

- ❤ Clear the weight if you feel heavy by taking time to feel the emotions.
- ❤ Journal—write about your feelings.
- ❤ Go to the bridge and hook onto them and express them.
- ❤ Release any toxic emotions.
- ❤ Feel the fear if you have any.
- ❤ Cry if you feel that you need to.
- ❤ Pound a pillow if you have anger.
- ❤ Stamp your feet if you are frustrated.
- ❤ Release the uncomfortable emotions.
- ❤ Reconnect with your own source of love and peace within.
- ❤ If you are triggered and you have to deal with inappropriate behavior with others.
- ❤ Get centered … Breathe.
- ❤ Protect your self-worth.
- ❤ Ask for clarity.
- ❤ Stand up for yourself.

To Trust is the first step to everything ...

To feel the energy and melt into the safeness of your own heart, embracing the unconditional love that protects each emotion as it is felt. The blueprint of the aspects of self and the direction of the journey is revealed. The mystery of the plan directs the soul's evolution as the human emotions are placed in the safe place to be acknowledged, owned, felt and released.

As the pain is felt the change of perception penetrates the experience so that spirit's surrender can be felt. The heart slowly opens to find its way to the self-love. This part of the heart that has been closed has waited for this moment of love.

As I assist in co-creating a safe place for this experience, the vibration is lifted higher and higher until we let go of our heaviness, the density that keeps us from that part of ourselves. The place we have no frame of reference for, this place of divine love when we feel the flow of our destiny and the truth of why we are here. No barriers, just freedom to be all that we are.

We have crossed through the passage of resistance and the energy of strength and source flows through our every cell, as we remember who we are. Our purpose has been revealed as we sit in the bliss of the moment, no past or future. This knowingness exists once we have let go of all attachments to the outcome, arriving at the moment of creation in us.

Our self-worth leads us to more love and our self-love lifts our self-worth to a higher vibration. This experience is the awakening of our life force and the realization of our perfection and uniqueness.

Colleen Hoffman Smith

Inner Peace

Formula 1 – **Inner Relationship**—Reconnecting with our self-love, guiding us to our inner connection and a safe relationship with our emotions.

Formula 2 – **Inner Workout**—Teaches us how to embrace our toxic anger and heavy emotions healthily, to clear the way for peace, to empty ourselves of our fears and uncomfortable feelings and find our way back to our connection of self-love and self-worth.

Formula 3 – **Inner Peace**—Is the result of practicing Formulas 1 and 2. Peace is the result and this takes us into our life without expectations, attachment, judgment or blame.

Inner Peace is a place inside that feels absolutely wonderful. In this place,

LOVE JUST IS,

and we can feel our calmness and connection to everything inside us and out.

In this place of peace we can trust that God or the universe has a better plan than we have. We can be prepared for anything. This wisdom and trust keeps me committed to my practice of staying connected to my own self-worth.

Once you have the practice and the formulas woven in your life you can know instantly when you feel uncomfortable. This is when you can go inside, to the emotion, which is asking for attention.

ANY FEELING, OTHER THAN PEACE AND LOVE,

AWAKENS ALL OF YOUR SENSES TO REMIND YOU

THAT THERE IS SOMETHING BLOCKING THE WAY

TO YOUR PEACE.

GO TO THE BRIDGE

TO YOUR INNER CHILD RELATIONSHIP

AND CREATE A

SAFE PLACE.

Once you feel connected to your safe relationship within, bring any other person or experience that is triggering your uncomfortable feelings. Once you clear the heaviness or the darkness, you can find your way back to self-love, self-worth and peace. Everyone you connect with will feel this inner connection to your peace.

When you are centered and feeling peace, you are in the present and free to make choices, stay focused and take action. Instead of reacting with our emotions, peace guides us in making choices. When centered we can easily focus. We are ready to take action in peace and love, not anger or fear.

When I lived in fear, anger or sadness, I didn't even like answering the phone or greeting a new day. I didn't feel good unless people or experiences made me feel good or took me out of my uncomfortable way of existing. When I felt great I went around trying to make everyone else feel good. It was exhausting.

Now that I am connected to my own peace and self-worth, I feel different. When dark feelings threaten, I face those feelings and recognize that this uncomfortable experience or person is the messenger that will bring me to my unfelt emotions or my lack of self-worth.

When doing my daily practice, I feel that I have more control over myself. Life is more peaceful because I am. My behavior is different because I feel more in touch with each moment. The clearer I become, the easier it is to continue this practice of expanding from the inside. This peace in me has no judgment or blame, no anger or fear, and this is why people feel safe with me. This peace in me attracts people. They want to be with me because I feel comfortable with myself: therefore, they feel comfortable. If someone misbehaves or feels uncomfortable I can remember the place in me when I misbehaved because of my unfelt emotions. From this place of compassion I can then be with someone authentically, speaking truth and inspiring others to feel that part in themselves if they choose. When I am centered and in this place of peace, believing in myself, it is easy to see when others cannot feel it in themselves.

Peace is the fountain of youth and each day I practice and find it easier. Feeling this connection in me lightens me instead of feeling tired all the time because I carried around so much heaviness. People say that I keep looking younger. The truth is I feel younger and more alive. My healthy spirit, mind and body need constant attention, but now that I am more present I have this relationship with myself everyday ... all day. This relationship does not interfere with anything; this connection enhances everything. I believe that the more connected I am to my moments, the more present I am to see the openings in my world of opportunity.

I experience a wonderful part of myself each time I go to my emotions and deal with them. If I am sick, my body usually tells me that there are some issues or emotions that need to be embraced. A wonderful book that confirms my own body talk is *Heal Your Body* by Louise Hay. This quick guide and reference book explains how unfelt emotions and issues might create some of our illnesses. It's another way to have an intimate and caring relationship with yourself. Each emotional or physical trauma took me to my relationship with myself. Each time I was feeling unsure of myself or in fear, I went inside. In the beginning, I went there frequently, to the bridge, where I learned to truthfully feel and find my way back to my self-worth, and self-love. Each time I came out of it I felt better. I felt more expanded within and there was more room for peace and love. There was more space inside so that I could love more. This calmness and wonderful feeling of connection inside me strengthened and expanded more and more into my day.

One day I woke up and compared my life that day to the life I had lived up to this time. What was different? I felt different. It was **Peace.** I realized that by living this way I had attracted a new life of peace and love, but what was different was that it was coming from inside of me. Now that I owned all of my misbehaviors and uncomfortable emotions I felt the difference in me. You can too! When you have connected with your peace and you are living it, you will not have to prove anything to anyone. You will not have to put anyone down or criticize anyone or anything any longer to make yourself feel better. You won't have to take up all the space in a room to feed your insecurities. You will feel safe to listen and to feel and it will be easier to be the silent witness when someone misbehaves. You can then be centered enough to speak with truth and words that will inspire others. Your energy and body language will be more authentic and attractive. When you are in Peace the fear is gone. When you feel peace you have healthily taken care of your anger. Your Peace embraces your self-worth and you feel confident. Inner Peace creates a safe place for you and others. Your Peace is the pathway to the love in you.

LOVE HEALS EVERYTHING

— ❤ —

Meditation for when a person or experience triggers you out of your Peace.

Close your eyes. Breathe deeply and bring your attention to your root chakra, the place where your passion sits. The fire burns here in your womanhood or manhood, your genital area. Breathe deeply and connect to this energy. This is your life force … your sexual energy. If you cannot feel it, try to see it in your mind's eye. Ignite it by seeing the electricity or the fire. Know it is there. It is always there.

Visualize this energy and feel it. Lift this energy up with your breath, up into your solar plexus (just below your rib cage). Put your hand on your heart and feel the inner connection.

See the bridge between the worlds, the bridge between this world and paradise, between past and present ... see the bridge. As you walk on the bridge feel yourself and be aware of what is around you. Create a beautiful paradise, the place that makes you feel good, feel safe.

When you feel safe, see yourself when you were a child walking towards you (your inner child). Relax into this safe relationship and feel the love. Make sure your inner child feels safe. Bring the experience, person, or people with whom you want to heal, out onto the bridge. Feel the energy of the person and the experience. Be aware of any emotions like anger, fear or loneliness and tell these people how you feel. Pound a pillow, cry, talk about it ... whatever you feel ... let it out. This is the healthy place to do it. This is the place to practice with this energy and to find your way back to peace. See their behavior as separate from yours and find the compassion to forgive if you can. Stay until you and your inner child feel safe with them or the experience. Practice this until you feel you have your uncomfortable emotions out of your body. Find your way back to love, love your child inside and love yourself.

Eventually you will be able to stay in your peace the next time this person or experience with the same energy comes into your space. Practice on the bridge telling this person how you feel. You can stand up to the bully and not go to reaction or lose your power. You can practice asking for what you need. You can practice finding your way back to your own self-worth and not losing your powerful connection to source. No one is your source of strength and love. Don't give your source or power away to anyone. This connection is always waiting for you within.

Inner Peace Summary

- ❤ Inner Peace is a result of practicing Formulas 1 and 2.

- ❤ The commitment to your relationship, to yourself and how you feel.

- ❤ The result is peace in you and your life.

- ❤ To be free to be all that you are, without the influence of past hurts and future attachments.

- ❤ Peace is inspiring.

The Message in the Space

The beauty of space within attracts the miracle of life,
birthed in each moment without our control.
The harmony of our breath ...
without the interference of details and struggle,
make way for the space that is already there.

Take the time to walk with this space,
inside and outside of us.
Be in this place,
and feel the nothingness of everything.
Lift our own vibration to the level
where we have no mind.

The picture of the present
is the space that is like a canvas.
With the unfolding of the picture as you breathe ...
the light and dark, giving birth
to the colors that are brilliant,
because the love has pulled the emotions
from the empty space to be felt.

As the picture unfolds,
the present moment embraces the masterpiece of peace.

Colleen Hoffman Smith

CHAPTER THREE

LEAD From Yourself

The Head and Heart Connection

I have experienced leadership that uses control and manipulation. I have seen leaders who react out of fear and self-doubt, who forget about their heart.

When our head and heart meet in a relationship, we are brought into the present and feel connected to everything around us. This relationship between our head and our heart allows us to be in a place where our intellect and feelings merge, creating the wisdom to make choices without fear. If we don't use our heart when making decisions, our head can keep us stuck in distractions or in wounds from the past or fear of the future, holding us in self-doubt or dysfunctional behavior.

Our heart reminds us of who we are, restores our self-worth and keeps us connected and committed to the strength of our relationship within. This experience opens us up to fully connect with our inner peace and strength, freeing us to be fully aware of our personal and professional relationships and experiences. To be all that we can be, free of fear and self-doubt.

INSPIRE FROM YOUR TRUE SELF

WHEN ARE YOU NOT AN INSPIRATION?

L ❤❤ K AT ME

I AM SUCH A GOOD ACTOR

SO GOOD THAT I **F O O L** **MYSELF**

THAT'S WHY YOU CAN'T FEEL ME!!

I CAN'T FEEL ME!!!!

Being a leader might be a role you're given or a position that has been handed to you. You might be extremely well paid to lead or manage people. However, I believe that the more connected you are to yourself and the more comfortable you are, the better you will lead and inspire others. I have seen leadership in a person who is not recognized by title or salary. Leadership occurs where there is inspiration from within, when you have self-worth and are at peace.

If your boss or manager is not an inspiring leader, it should not stop you from being one. You can inspire anyone by being true to yourself, and being connected to all that you are. When you are clear of the heavy emotions, you are then free to be yourself, present and comfortable.

Drew was having a lot of difficulties in his marriage and with his job. He was vice-president of a large national organization. He found leadership very hard and knew that his staff did not really like him. He felt it when he entered meetings, either with a group or one-on-one. He had a lot of fears and self-worth issues and his communication skills were poor. As he shared his daily experiences at home and at work with me, I could feel the anger between his words. He had no tolerance for others and he liked to control everything. Although his ego and controlling personality seemed to always get him somewhere in life, he now felt that something was missing. People would shut down from him and he felt that he had lost his power over them. The people who worked under his leadership didn't respond to him candidly and he felt lonely. He didn't feel safe and there seemed to be division in his team. Drew's marriage was not feeling comfortable either. His wife felt like a stranger and he felt her anger a great deal; he couldn't seem to do anything right in her eyes.

My first comment to him was that it was great that he was feeling something and was aware of what was going on in his life. I also explained to him that this behavior around him had probably been there for a long time, but now that he was awake to it, he felt uncomfortable. The experiences were bringing him inside himself. I felt a lot of anger from Drew and felt that this anger was getting so large that he couldn't contain it any longer. This was why people felt uncomfortable. The anger was what was waking him up.

As he started to talk about his childhood, it became clear to both of us that his anger had been suppressed since he was a little boy. He didn't know how to deal with it. The women in the family (grandmothers, aunts, mother) raised him, filling him up all the time. There was no shortage of love and things to make him happy. He was the talented, good-looking boy that brought them so much love. He became the "dancing bear" for the whole family, bringing them joy and love constantly. They praised him and rewarded him for being so great. They felt so good when he was around. He was the light in their life.

Drew had no relationship with his father and felt he could never make his father proud of him. Drew's father was shut down and controlling. His mother didn't have an easy time with his father either. She could never stand up to him and she constantly behaved like a victim, always taking care of everyone but herself.

Drew felt his anger as he took responsibility for his experiences. He was angry for not having his father's approval and love, and angry at his mother for not standing up for herself. As he owned his anger and felt it on the bridge, he allowed his inner child to scream and cry with pain. He became humble and vulnerable. As he released this pain from his body he could feel a sense of peace. This is when he forgave his parents, realizing it wasn't up to them to give him his love—he had to find it in himself. Even though his father had died years before, he could do this healing on the bridge and forgive both his parents. He realized they were doing their best and loving him the only way they knew how.

I guided Drew to the bridge where he could go back to his memories when he was a child, hooking into the energy of the experiences with his father. He could feel the unworthiness that he had felt with his Dad. He could feel the emptiness, his anger and fear. He allowed his inner child to feel the pain. As he held onto the anger, he allowed his body to release it …he cried and yelled at his father. He released the pain from his body and then he became clear and peaceful, saw that his father was shut down himself and not embracing his own anger and fear…not feeling his self-worth or self-love.

Drew saw how he had become his father in many ways. The parts that he hated in his father were in him. As he forgave his father, he had to embrace these parts in himself. Drew also forgave his mother for not loving herself. He saw that he shut down with his wife because she was no different than his mother…a victim energy…not loving herself. His mother was afraid of his father's control and she filled Drew up with lots of love to feel good. Drew's father probably felt jealous of the love his mother gave to her son. Drew saw how his mother's victim energy closed him, yet her giving, filling-up nature made him feel good. His mother also loved others and took care of everyone to get the love for herself.

Because Drew was shut down, his wife could not feel him or his love. Drew realized that he really didn't have a lot of respect for women because of his past conditioning. His attitude and energy around women was very condescending and self-righteous when he didn't respect them. Drew now recognized how he would become judgmental when he felt a needy or victim energy (like his mother's) in women he associated with.

I told him that he couldn't fix his wife or anyone else. But if he started to take care of his uncomfortable emotions he would become more open, and his wife and other people would be able to feel his open heart.

Drew's healing with his mother happened when he changed his perception. He brought his mother onto the bridge and he became compassionate and saw her hidden potential and her weakness. He felt the guilt that he had carried all these years of not loving that part in her, and how he shut down from her, not loving her unconditionally. As he felt the pain, he was moved to a deep respect. This was the opening for him to change his behavior with others—forgiving his parents and changing his mind. He could feel a huge space inside, it was beautiful to see him as he released.

Drew's inauthentic and unattractive behavior came from a life of pretending and trying to contain all of his judgments, blame, anger and fear. Drew's marriage did not mend for many reasons. The damage was too great and when there is a lot of hurt and dysfunction, sometimes each party needs to find a safe place to heal. It takes two people to make or break a relationship …both have to show up, heal the past, live in the present and continue to hold the space for the other.

FINDING THE LOVE

OF YOU STARTS FROM

AND THEN
THE INNER LOVE ATTRACTS

Drew's career and relationships are changing and his new perception about himself has taken him to new places of peace and pain. His leadership is more inspiring and his professional relationships more meaningful. Drew feels more authentic with others and a lot more connected to himself. His relationship with his ex-wife is evolving into a wonderful friendship. He is more comfortable with her and his children. Drew is inspiring his children to be more present and connected to truth and inner love. His energy has changed in his leadership role as a vice-president of a national company. His behavior is more *Authentic, Attractive* and *Inspiring*.

WHAT MAKES A GOOD LEADER
SO GREAT!!!

- A leader has a vision woven with a higher purpose.
- A leader inspires others to find the place inside themselves that inspires. One light lighting another.
- There is no control or greed in a good leader.
- They have found the peace in themselves and they don't need anything from anyone.
- They are humble because they have been to the places of pain inside where we have all been or are going.
- There is no judgment in a good leader, just a strong belief in themselves and others.
- A good leader has no hidden agenda.
- Integrity is woven into their essence.
- A good leader is compassionate and sees each person as an equal.
- You can feel the passion of a good leader as they talk about a mission or their purpose.
- You feel safe with a good leader.
- They are authentic and easy to be with.

- A good leader is comfortable with themselves and others.
- A good leader could be anyone who can inspire another to be all that they are.
- They can walk into any experience, any room knowing who they are.
- A good leader is the example of strength, peace and courage.
- A good leader has taken the time to mend their broken heart.
- They have taken care of their own emotional body, allowing their true nature to shine.
- They are open and connected to each experience, taking themselves out of the way, letting go of the attachment to the outcome.
- The joy is in them; therefore they create a great experience.
- They are attractive people because they are connected to their own self-worth
- Good leaders are real people believing and trusting in others.
- They create their future from peace, not fear.
- **A GOOD LEADER BECOMES A GREAT LEADER AS THEY INSPIRE FROM WITHIN.**

Give *and* Receive

TO **BE** THE LOVE ...

Instead of giving the love.

TO **FEEL** THE LOVE ...

Instead of receiving the love.

— ❤ —

I believe that when giving and receiving, we should pay attention to our intention within the act. Giving love so that people feel good distracts them from feeling their own pain. Receiving love is a distraction when we are in pain, because we are feeling another's love instead of feeling our uncomfortable pain and moving into our own love inside.

BE the Love

For us to be in love and at peace inside, is to *be* the love inspiring another to make a choice to feel it in themselves... to remember their own love and peace.

When someone we love is in pain, our first instinct may be to try to make our loved one feel good by giving away our love and light, or, we may shut down and not love ourselves. Holding the space for them, allowing them to feel their own pain, gives them an opportunity to do their own practice. We can inspire them by loving ourselves and being sincere, creating a safe place for them to move their pain out of the way. I like to visualize a lamp on a table. If I am that lamp, I can be turned on, thereby creating light, or I could be turned off, plunging everything into darkness.

A relationship becomes very difficult if you have to fill up someone constantly. It is a huge responsibility to make people feel love or feel good. It can also be very controlling on our part if we fill people up and try to fix another. To let go of our control is to love and honor another person's choice of process for healing on their journey through life. You can spend the time and energy on yourself, showing others your healthy lifestyle instead of having others look to you to feel good, to feel love inside. **BE the love** and inspire others, instead of giving it away.

Loving another is to be the love by......

Sharing time, showing love, being calm, being present, giving your attention, listening, caring, believing in someone, sharing abundance, laughing, giving solace, being authentic, speaking truthfully, being in love without conditions ... these are all ways to give from a full heart.

FEEL the Love

Receiving is very different from taking. Sometimes it's exhausting being with someone who demands a lot of attention, needy for your love to be happy or fulfilled. Someone like this doesn't like to be alone and takes from you. Usually a needy person can never really be happy with what you give them. Remember, their emptiness is not your responsibility to fill. The best you can do for this relationship is not give yourself away.

When someone is in pain, or looks to others for love, they cannot truly feel the love unless they have connected to their own love inside. The gift of feeling love is a lot more powerful than giving it or taking it.

WE CANNOT RECEIVE IT UNLESS
WE RECOGNIZE IT *IN OURSELVES.*

LOVE IS IN EVERYONE

Bring yourself to a memory of when you were incredibly stressed, in your head or in your pain. If someone at this time gives you solace, supporting you emotionally, creating a safe place and reminder of peace … this love can be felt if we choose to find that place in us to feel it. Can we be present with ourselves, so that we can receive kindness without guilt or feel the relationship without conditions?

When we do our own practice daily with Formulas 1, 2 and 3, we can find our way to

- ❤ **BE the Love and FEEL the Love**.
- ❤ **BEing the love** is giving a gift of our present connection to self.
- ❤ **FEELing the love** is receiving a gift from our present connection to self.

If we can practice "living present" and connected to our own self-love and self-worth, we can be the gift of inspiration for the children, our family and friends. We can inspire our professional life from this place inside that has no judgment or control.

Practice not to compare yourself with anyone ... we are all unique and powerful. Think of each person in your life as your brother or sister, no different than you. Realize that everyone who is misbehaving is reacting from their lack of connection to their self-worth. Inspire others by Leading from Yourself ... the person who you have discovered, the one who has the strength and courage to face all of your fears and uncomfortable emotions each day ... to be centered and clear to find your way back to Peace and Self-Love.

Lead and Inspire from YOURSELF

Conclusion

You will find that as you do this practice with the formulas, you can get to a level of peace and self-worth. This place in you that makes you feel better than you did before. Time in this joyous place will then bring you to a new level of emotions that need to be felt. You will find that you will have to be with those feelings again and again. Each time you clear the heaviness, you will feel more expanded. There will be more peace and more love. You will attract a better life. I believe that I will be doing this practice until the end of my days. I pray that I will never stop. I feel blessed to feel love and peace in my life, and each level of emotional work I embrace brings me to an even better place in me.

Take the time to LOOK inside to discover yourself. LIVE to be yourself, to be more authentic and attractive by taking care of your emotional body. Clear the heaviness by doing your Inner Workout whenever you need to, to find your way back to Inner Peace. LEAD from yourself by being the example and inspiring others. Create a wonderful life and a beautiful future.

— ❤ —

This practice has been woven into my life for almost nine years now. From the experience of living my HELL, I created formulas and practiced each day to find my way back to peace "inside me" where love lives. I have surrounded myself with people who desire the same for themselves and support me each day. I have attracted a wonderful life. You can too! I am no different from you! *Pocket Guide to your He❤rt* is the path that you can walk to a rich and fulfilling life. It just takes practice.

More about ...
Pocket Guide to your He♥rt

Colleen's *Pocket Guide to your He♥rt* formulas have been a great inspiration to me, giving me all the tools I need to find peace and contentment in my life. Never before have I come across one single program that could help me accomplish so much. It is something I can refer to over and over again to maintain a balance in my life that I never dreamed was possible.

Bettina Mann, Desktop Publisher

Colleen is truly a messenger of love. Her work has been instrumental in guiding me to create a safe space and open up to the peace and joy within my heart.

Karen King, Corporate Coach

Never in my entire 51 years of roaming this entire planet from corner to corner, have I encountered anyone or anything that has so quickly, easily and comfortably brought me to a place where I can visit anytime and anywhere to connect with who I am and what makes me happy and peaceful.

Rick Gavey, Marketing Executive

Pocket Guide to your He♥rt formulas have greatly transformed my life and has become my daily practice to continue to develop a loving relationship with the most important person in my life...ME! As a result I have more open and connected relationships with everyone in my life, especially with my children. I am so grateful to have the opportunity to inspire them and others to go inside and find that center of love and self-worth within.

Jo-Anne Cutler, Business Manager, Life Coach

As a successful entrepreneur, Colleen has been instrumental in teaching me how I can shift my being to a state of inner peace and contentment. Initially I was very skeptical of the entire spiritual process and truly had to let go of preconceived notions that I was "just fine, thank you very much" as my logical mind told me anything spiritual was a bit flaky. I was wrong. Her ability to coach me to a balanced state of well being blending the logic of the mind with the intuition of the heart is phenomenal. "To show up" regardless of the circumstance and "to change your dance step" from existing long-term habits that haven't worked, is a skill that requires tremendous inner strength, and commitment. *Pocket Guide to your He♥rt* formulas are my personal tool that I will keep in my pocket.

ONLY THE FEAR OF THE UNKNOWN
GETS IN OUR WAY TO MOVING FORWARD
Brenda Atkinson, President, Atkinson Design Group

Colleen has taught me how to take responsibility, live authentically without fear and to love unconditionally.
I thank God every day for sending me to the best coach He has!
Nancy Newman, Artist, Poet and Teacher, Life Coach

Pocket Guide to your He♥rt is a powerful tool to connect to self, to learn how to constructively deal with anger and other emotions and to strive to find inner peace. Colleen's clear and simple techniques are helping me to become more authentic and attractive. Colleen taught me to connect to and have a positive relationship with my inner child. How important it is for her, even as an adult to feel safe, nurtured and loved. As a teacher and a parent how important is it for me to share these skills with the children I encounter in my life. Anyone who follows Colleen's formulas can truly begin to "create a wonderful life and a beautiful future."

Judy McDowell, Grade School Teacher

Colleen has brought us to the deepest place in our souls. *Pocket Guide to your He♥rt* formulas has helped us tremendously in our personal and professional lives. It is not often that you really connect with your past, present and future. We feel that Colleen provides a wonderful tool for gaining and establishing your true strength and love. The beauty of *Pocket Guide to your He♥rt* formulas is that it is not really a system to learn or memorize it is a simple technique to connect you with your inner self. Through this a great healing of past, present and future occurs.

Lily & Loris Colasanti, (R.M.T.'s)

Colleen came into my life at 'just the right time', which was, of course, when I was ready. After a number of years of working on my body-mind-soul connection, I was feeling stuck. By creating a safe place for me and helping me to recognize, truly feel and to work through my emotions, I am learning to love myself and to understand why certain people in my life trigger negative emotional responses. There is tremendous relief and joy in glimpsing the power within each of us that comes through unconditional love, accepting ourselves and others without judgment, as God intended. It is a process that gives me a different perspective on day-to-day events and the choices that I make. I am very grateful to have had this opportunity.

Sue Herd, Mother, Wife and Businesswoman

Coaching helps us to develop clarity about what is important to us and what we want out of life. *Pocket Guide to your He♥rt* offers a simple yet immediately effective technique to help clear the emotional blocks that prevents us from finding the meaning and focus we are all searching for. As we move through the three formulas—connecting with our inner relationship, doing our inner workout and finding our inner peace—we satisfy our primal need of creating intimacy with others. Thank you Colleen for providing a safe bridge to a successful pathway along the journey of life.

Lanee, Yoga Instructor

I had been grieving the loss of my boyfriend when I connected with Colleen.

I found the technique very easy to follow at home and use it daily. It helped me to uncover some blocks that had held me back my whole life. Being able to uncover them and address them has made an enormous difference in my life. For the first time, I am at peace with myself and am experiencing self love. My relationships with others have changed for the better because of the work I committed to do using *Pocket Guide to your He♥rt* formulas. I am finally able to feel my emotions and write about them. In so doing, I have been able to find serenity and joy in my life.

Barbara Lupton, Retired School Principal

Since our mom has known Colleen she has changed a lot! She doesn't yell anymore, she's happier, doesn't eat as much chocolate, smokes less (but not less enough!) she relaxes more, has lost weight (she says it's her emotions that were heavy), she cries over happy little things, has less wrinkles and sings and dances around the house even more than before. Thank you Colleen.

Brandon and Melissa (ages 10 and 12)

I have spent my entire life looking for love and trying to please others. Happiness was fleeting and contingent on external events. I had achieved success in many areas, but I always needed more and I had no peace in my life. Colleen and the *Pocket Guide to your He♥rt* techniques have transformed my life profoundly. I have found love inside myself, I find true happiness each and every day, and I have found peace. The relationship that my wife and I now share is awesome and we are both more effective parents. Thank-you Colleen I am truly grateful.

Mike Suffield, Assistant Vice President, CIT Financial

Practicing Colleen's formulas for living has inspired me to become my own best friend. Connecting with myself in this way has helped me discover a new source of power and beauty within. When my decision making came from this place, my life changed!

Linda Ginou. Mother of Five Children

When I read Colleen's book I hoped it would be another tool I could use on my journey of life. Little did I know it would turn out to be the only tool I would ever really need. With gratitude.

Robyn Moleiro, Television Spokesperson, Motivational Speaker, Life Coach

In a wonderfully warm environment Colleen's process skillfully guides you to your inner-self, teaching you how to love and hold yourself, so you have the care and comfort that you always wanted. Colleen confirms that the answer is within; we just all need to quiet our minds from the distractions on life, to love and heal our wounded selves.

Tricia Ryan, Partner, The Toolbox

Pocket Guide to your He♥rt promotes and supports the basis for sound company sales and footing from the inside out. Motivating from within and helping the individual is a key element of *The Pocket Coach*. Colleen has been able to verbalize through the pages of her book the need to take fear out of the equation and allow the individual to find their own comfort zone. Direct sales companies will benefit immensely by putting her techniques to use, and having her speak directly to the groups to motivate them with a positive message.

In Europe, the Caribbean and in the United States the goal of most individuals/companies is promoting their products through traditional sales and marketing techniques.

Unfortunately, many are driven by fear of failure, not properly motivated. There are a few companies with the insight to motivate by encouragement rather than negative input.

I believe *Pocket Guide to your He♥rt* to be one of the tools available to help blueprint a positive sales force, in particular in the direct sales arena.

Toby Coriell, Career Manager

About the Author

Colleen Hoffman Smith is an inspirational guide and facilitator. Her career experience in the fashion, modeling and the skin care world, woven with her desire to live authentically, helped her create three formulas to lighten the heart. Throughout her career she has learned important truths that she lives by. She understands the delicate balance between inner and outer attractiveness. She has found that the key to success lies in each personal journey to discover one's own self-worth and the confidence to overcome fears and anxieties.

Colleen believes that we can all attract a life of love and peace when we find it within. *Pocket Guide to your He♥rt* can be kept in your own pocket to assist you in becoming comfortable and content in your life, recognizing your unique self, where wisdom and deep truth is birthed.

Colleen facilitates *Pocket Guide to your He♥rt* seminars, workshops and one-on-one sessions.

We want to hear from you.

Colleen would love to hear how
Pocket Guide to your He♥rt has inspired you in
your professional or personal life. Please write her
with your stories, thoughts and successes
that you have experienced as a result of
reading this book.

E-mail your stories to:
edentrilogy@rogers.com

To order books in quantity or if you would like
to have one sent to a friend, visit our website at:
www.pocketguidetoyourheart.com

And for ...

Keynotes, Seminars
and Personal Coaching

Contact Jo-Anne Cutler at JC Connections
905-569-8334
or
email us at:
pocketguidetoyourheart@jcconnections.ca